The
Beader's Guide
to
Jewelry Design

Margie Deeb

The
Beader's Guide
to
Jewelry Design

A Beautiful Exploration
of Unity, Balance, Color & More

Margie Deeb

LARK JEWELRY
& BEADING

LARK JEWELRY & BEADING

An Imprint of Sterling Publishing
387 Park Avenue South
New York, NY 10016

ISBN 978-1-4547-0406-5

Library of Congress Cataloging-in-Publication Data

Deeb, Margie.
 The beader's guide to jewelry design : a beautiful exploration of unity, balance, color & more / Margie Deeb.
   pages cm
 Includes index.
 ISBN 978-1-4547-0406-5
 1. Beadwork. 2. Jewelry making. 3. Color in design. I. Title.
 TT860.D426 2014
 745.594'2--dc23
                2013037408

Distributed in Canada by Sterling Publishing
c/o Canadian Manda Group, 165 Dufferin Street
Toronto, Ontario, Canada M6K 3H6
Distributed in the United Kingdom by GMC Distribution Services
Castle Place, 166 High Street, Lewes, East Sussex, England BN7 1XU
Distributed in Australia by Capricorn Link (Australia) Pty. Ltd.
P.O. Box 704, Windsor, NSW 2756, Australia

For information about custom editions, special sales, and premium and corporate purchases, please contact Sterling Special Sales at 800-805-5489 or specialsales@sterlingpublishing.com.

Email academic@larkbooks.com for information about desk and examination copies. The complete policy can be found at larkcrafts.com.

Manufactured in China

2 4 6 8 10 9 7 5 3 1

larkcrafts.com

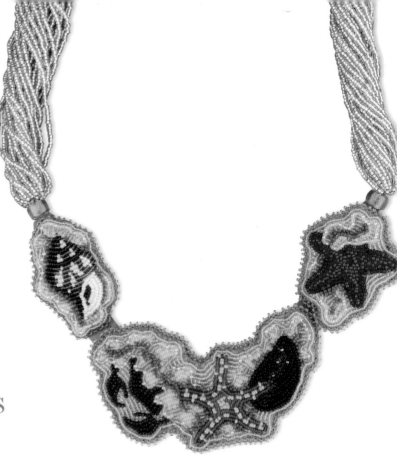

6 Color

7 Jewelry & the Body

8 The Creative Journey

Frieda Bates
Yasmine, 2010
35 x 17 x 2.5 cm
Dichroic glass cabs handmade
by artist, seed beads, faceted
glass beads, suede; bead
embroidery, stringing

Jewelry As Magic

We diminish the significance of jewelry—and its creation—when we consider it simply ornamentation. The very heart of jewelry is the expression of being. Each time we make and adorn ourselves with jewelry we give ourselves over to an ancient ritual, a ceremony where the alchemy of our creativity combines with the passion of our self-expression.

The result? Magic.

You've opened this book because, like me, you want to more fully understand that magic. So let's map a part of the terrain where jewelry's magic lies: design.

Why does a piece of jewelry make us feel more alive and in touch with our muse? Why are we sometimes amazed by our creations, and other times ready to toss them? Why, when we've followed every design concept, are our visions sometimes unfulfilled? We'll use our vision, our senses, and our intuition to explore these questions. In creating jewelry, as in life, when we pay deep attention we come closer to knowing ourselves and how we relate to our world. We understand why we've chosen jewelry as our sacred medium of self-expression.

Many of the pieces I've chosen that illustrate specific design principles also appear in *Showcase 500 Beaded Jewelry* (Lark Crafts, 2012). This book is, to date, the most outstanding compilation of contemporary beaded jewelry available. And It's a valuable resource for observing and studying the field at large. The artists whose work is contained within its pages, as well as those online and in the global beading community, have been generous in sharing their work with me. Their extraordinary contributions bring the beauty, theory, and concepts we're exploring to life.

The Beader's Guide to Jewelry Design was created with the input of online friends and readers. When I asked questions in my newsletter and through social media, you responded. Throughout these pages you'll see names of those, perhaps yourself, who responded to my questions. I am very grateful for your input.

May you weave creativity and magic into every area of your life.

Margie Deeb

1 | Unity

Designers are creative fire starters, our inner worlds simmering with ideas, images, and visions. Turning our hot nova visions into jewelry requires us to make creative decisions that are not only intuitive, but also conscious and informed. When you remain aware of the principles of design in these pages, aiming always for balance of unity and variety, your jewelry will sparkle with the starry-eyed passion that fueled it.

Every good design expresses visual harmony—harmony in which every part affirms its connection with all the rest, each element speaking to and with the other. Color, placement, texture, pattern, technique, materials, and components belong together: They're related to each other and to the whole. There's an intentional order and purpose to the piece. We call this kind of harmony *unity*.

THE BIG PICTURE

The most important aspect of visual unity is the big picture: perceiving the whole piece before you notice individual elements (figure 1-1). This concept is called the *gestalt* of

Figure 1-1   When you look at a beautifully unified design you see the overall necklace first. In this case, a radiant starburst of gold and copper captures your attention and draws you in, compelling you to look closer and discover bullets.

Rebecca Starry
High Caliber Collar, 2009
30.5 x 25.4 x 1.9 cm
Seed beads, accent beads, assorted caliber bullets, assorted findings, beading thread, wire; right angle weave, embellished
PHOTO BY JESSICA STEPHENS

Figure 1-2 **Patricia Zabreski Venaleck**
Purple Rain, 2009
50.8 x 2.5 x 1.3 cm
Handmade lampworked glass lentil beads, crystal leaves, crystals; stringing
PHOTO BY JERRY ANTHONY

Figure 1-3
Margie Deeb
Untitled, 2010
7 x 4 cm
Seed beads, enamel, silver; square stitch

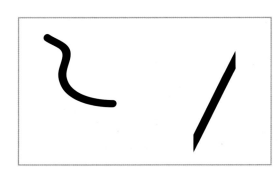

Figure 1-4

a work of art. Gestalt theory holds that the whole is more than the sum of its parts. Consider a melody. You can't understand a melody by simply examining its notes. The melody is comprised of the notes in their specific placement, sustained for specific duration. And yet, the melody is much more than the notes and their placement. Therefore the melody is not simply the sum of its parts, but a synergistic "whole effect," or gestalt.

The same is true of jewelry. An exquisitely designed piece of jewelry expresses far more than the beads and patterns that form it. Because of the unity of its design it is first and foremost a necklace (figure 1-2) or pair of earrings (figure 1-3), and then beads, colors, and patterns.

Achieving this level of unity can be a challenge for some beaders, especially those who delight in making complex components. The tendency is to focus on the intricacy of the component, not the aesthetics of the overall piece or its visual unity. Focusing on components only, they neglect the impact of overall effect, the big picture. If the first thing you notice when looking at a beaded necklace is the collection of intricately woven components rather than a beautiful cohesive piece of jewelry, you're witnessing a lack of unity of design.

WIRED FOR VISUAL UNITY

Lucky for us designers, nature is on our side. Humans are always looking for coherent visual relationships. That's the way we're wired. When the eye sees two lines within a specified area it will try to connect them or figure out how they're related (figure 1-4).

Whether we're viewing a painting, the interior of a room, or a piece of jewelry, our brain looks for relationships. We don't want to see confusion. We like unity and are drawn to a coherent pattern. If we can't find it, chances are we'll ignore what we see and move on. The fact that people innately seek visual unity makes our job of creating it easier.

Unity is the goal of good design: how *much* unity is the challenge. Valerie Fimple told me she "doesn't know when to say when" regarding how much variety to include within a piece of jewelry. Playing it safe too often, Donna Davis is frustrated by her overuse of similarity. Both are facing the same challenge of how to balance variety and repetition in order to create striking unity.

Think of unity not as a destination, but as a state existing somewhere between random variety and repetitious uniformity. Look at the spectrum in the line illustration below (figure 1-5). To help us understand unity in jewelry design, I've concocted the Unitometer (figure 1-6).

On the left—the random variety end of the spectrum—is jewelry made of beads with different sizes, shapes, and colors. On the right—the repetitious uniformity end—is jewelry composed of beads that are similar or the same. The illustrated strand of beads changes from random variety to repetitious uniformity.

The Unitometer will help you assess the degree of uniformity among the elements in a piece of jewelry. Understand, however, that there is a difference between "unity" and "uniformity." We are *not* aiming for uniformity, in which all elements are the same.

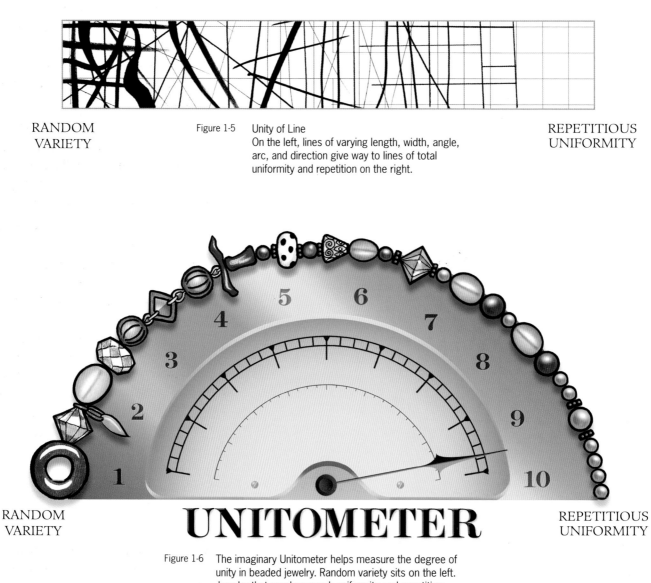

RANDOM
VARIETY

Figure 1-5   Unity of Line
On the left, lines of varying length, width, angle, arc, and direction give way to lines of total uniformity and repetition on the right.

REPETITIOUS
UNIFORMITY

RANDOM
VARIETY

UNITOMETER

REPETITIOUS
UNIFORMITY

Figure 1-6   The imaginary Unitometer helps measure the degree of unity in beaded jewelry. Random variety sits on the left. Jewelry that employs much uniformity and repetition earns a higher, but not neccessarily better, number.

Illustration by Margie Deeb and iStockphoto/CagriOner

Figure 1-7 This exploration of texture and beads falls on the left end of the unity scale, somewhere between 1 and 2. Some unity is present within the color, but variety and randomness prevail.

SaraBeth Cullinan
Untitled, 2010
19.5 x 3.8 cm
Seed and bugle beads, crystals, glass pearls; peyote and ladder stitch

Repeat, repeat, repeat! Size, color, shape, materials... all are repeated. Such abundant repetition places this necklace on the right end of the Unitometer, between 9 and 10, and creates beautiful harmony.

Debra Evans-Paige
Sunrise on Sand, 2006
50.5 x 5.9 x 1.5 cm
Stoneware, porcelain, sterling silver, silk; hand formed, textured, oxidation and reduction fired, hammered, knotted

We are aiming instead for unity found by striking an exquisite balance of variety and repetition. One end of the spectrum is not better than the other. Regardless of how varied or uniform your jewlery designs are, they must possess that aesthetic balance. The balance is unique to each piece—that's where your creativity comes in.

Where on the Unitometer do your tastes land? Are you a bohemian who prefers the boisterous variety of the random end? Or are you a conservative who prefers the sleek design of the repetitious end?

Knowing where your customer's taste falls on the Unitometer will help you tailor jewelry to her liking. It's relatively easy to determine where someone's fashion sense lands on the Unitometer. How much do their clothing, accessories, and hair tend to match or coordinate? Think of friends and family: What rating would you give their tastes on the Unitometer?

Look at the four variations of Carol Dean Sharpe's *Ribbed Cuff Peyote Bracelet* on page 28. Because they each employ a different degree of variety and repetition, they fall at slightly different positions on the Unitometer.

The lack of uniformity in beadwork can be a liability. When random, non-related shapes, sizes, and colors are sewn together in a haphazard fashion, there isn't enough unity to create harmonious design (figure 1-7). This isn't an indictment of the free-form technique, but rather an easily graspable example of where unity can be introduced to create more harmonious, wearable jewelry. If your free-form is more "free" than "form" and you want to change that, move it to the right end of the Unitometer by repeating elements (see next page). When the artist using free-form techniques finds a cohesive way to relate a hodge-podge of elements, a successful work of wearable art is born.

Let's explore the main ways to achieve unity. You've used many of these, but perhaps without conscious awareness of how they contribute to unified design.

Repeating elements within a design is one of the easiest ways to achieve unity. We respond to the echo of repeated elements and the pattern they naturally make, such as the repetition of petals in a flower. Great songs rely on repetition of selected lyrics and refrains. Too much repetition, however, becomes tedious uniformity. The same lyrics and melody repeated too often (think "99 Bottles of Beer on the Wall") appeals to no one, except, perhaps, the inebriated.

Marcia DeCoster's *Victoria* is a beautiful example of complex, sophisticated repetition that continually delights the eye (figure 1-8).

Countless elements are available for us to repeat in beaded jewelry. To stir your imagination, a selection of these concepts is illustrated on page 15.

Figure 1-8   Repeated curves are the dominant unifying element in this piece. Repetition of components, drops, and 4-pointed crosses further unify the design. The variation of half-curves rotated and joined to form an exquisite oval-shaped point of focus brings the design to beautiful culmination.

Marcia DeCoster
Victoria, 2008
45.7 x 15.2 x 0.6 cm
Seed beads, crystal, fire polish,
Czech glass drops; right angle weave

Elements Available for Repetition in the Quest for Unity

Size Use the same size beads or components made from beads.

Shape Repeat bead, element, or component shape.

Color Repeat colors, similar colors, or similarly saturated colors.

Texture Repeat similarly textured elements and materials.

Pattern Repeat patterns identically or vary the size.

Theme Repeat motifs, such as a floral theme, to create conceptual unity.

Motif Repeat motifs, such as sea creatures, to create conceptual unity.

Materials Use similar materials, such as cut crystals or ceramic beads.

Direction Position beads and components, especially those with pointed ends, in the same direction.

Terry Kluytmans hoped to understand the difference between elegant simplicity and boring, lifeless design.

This is an important issue to explore, because too much repetition can indeed be visually boring. In a strand of pearls, the precise repetition of size, shape, color, and materials makes the piece uniform and predictable. A strand of pearls is considered supremely elegant. Is it boring and lifeless? What if the pearls didn't have the warm luster finish, but rather a flat, dull finish? Would it be as elegant?

This is subjective territory. Elegant simplicity lies in the eye of the beholder. Boring and lifeless is more easily agreed upon, and easier to detect.

Surprisingly, variety is also a method of achieving unity. Trees abound with very similar branches, yet none are exactly alike. If they were, we would not be as fascinated by them. Our eye delights in discovering relationships within the spice of variety. Change but one aspect, like the size of repeating elements, and you'll create a much more interesting piece while maintaining a high degree of unity (figure 1-9).

Variety creates intrigue and dynamism. Unity holds it together. What to vary is easy: Refer back to the design elements illustrated on page 15 and change things up in any of the categories. But how much do you change? Aye, there's the rub! The challenge for every designer is knowing how much variety to incorporate to create excitement and intrigue while retaining overall unity.

Each time you change something in your design you create variety. Here are a few more sophisticated approaches.

• **Slight Variations** A subtle but unexpected change within a piece composed of similar elements appeals to us. For example, a focal point might be the same element as the rest of the piece, but larger (or smaller). Slight variations invite the viewer to come closer and explore (figure 1-10).

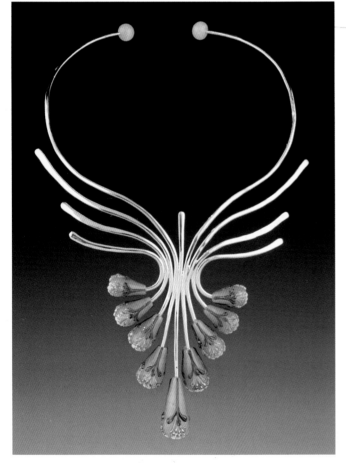

Figure 1-9   Variations in size add interest to the repetition of color, shape, line, and texture. Such uniformity rates high on the unity scale.

Patricia Zabreski Venaleck
Wings of Flight, 2009
0.3 x 2 x 3.3 cm
Handmade lampwork beads and forged, soldered silver wire
PHOTO BY JERRY ANTHONY

Figure 1-10   Repetition of circular shapes and similar colors unifies the design, opening the door for variety in the center of each disc.

Marcie Stone
Antique Pearl Button Necklace, 2011
0.5 x 15.5 x 18.5 cm
Seed beads, antique buttons, glass cabochons; peyote stitch
PHOTO BY GREG HANSON

Figure 1-11

Jeannette Cook
May's Garden Necklace, 2007
76 x 14 x 3 cm
Cylinder and seed beads,
Lucite flowers, pressed glass
beads, coral beads; right angle
weave, variations on peyote
stitch, daisy chain, surface
embellishment, stringing

- **Extreme Contrast** Push variety to the extremes of polar opposites: combine profuse texture with smooth surfaces; curved shapes with straight edges; deep darks with bright, light hues. Strongly contrasting elements are related in that they are opposites. They beckon the viewer to find that relationship. The piece is unified in its depiction of the contrast it represents (figure 1-11).

- **Emphasizing Variety** Variety can be the thrust of a design. This is the objective of some free-form beading. You may opt to create a piece that superficially appears uncontrolled and chaotic. However, you'll still need some degree of unity to pull it all together. The jewelry on this page shows extreme contrast and variety. Because the designers chose to repeat select elements or motifs, they each display beautiful unity (figures 1-11 through 1-13).

Figure 1-12

Susan Lenart Kazmer
Talisman, 2007
17.8 cm
Glass beads, brass, copper,
sterling, stainless steel found
objects, steel wire, rivets,
mica, plastic; antiquing,
drilling, wire wrapping
PHOTO BY STEWART O'SHIELDS

Figure 1-13

Stephanie Sersich
Summer Necklace, 2009
21 x 23 x 1.5 cm
Handmade glass beads, abalone, Roman glass, Lucite,
recycled glass and Czech glass beads; knotted with perle
cotton and waxed linen
PHOTO BY TOM EICHLER

Proximity

In the night sky we locate a constellation by the proximity of its stars (figure 1-14). The relationship of those stars to each other and to the space surrounding them becomes a recognizable design. There is unity within that constellation. Placing elements close together creates unity.

When placed farther apart, elements have less relation to each other: we perceive multiple, disparate items. Distance reinforces their differences (figure 1-15).

When elements are in proximity to one another, the eye—always looking for visual relationships—perceives them as related (figure 1-16). It interprets elements in proximity as a total pattern. For example, your eye immediately perceives a relationship between a caption placed close to a photo.

Jewelry is relatively small, so elements placed within it are in proximity. They are naturally related to one another because they share a small area defined as, say, a necklace.

Proximity alone, however, does not create harmonious unity. Precise attention must be paid to how elements relate to each other, especially in small spaces. Proximity must be used deliberately and elements arranged carefully so they visually unite. The goal is for the viewer's eye to move effortlessly from one element to the next.

Figure 1-14   We recognize the Big Dipper constellation because of proximity: how close the stars are to each other.

Figure 1-15   Because these elements are placed without proximity they are more likely to be perceived as six separate beads.

Figure 1-16   When elements are given close proximity, a degree of unity occurs. Notice how your eye perceives the beads within each group as related.

Cluster Creatively Clustering the colored beads together in the center unifies and brings them more attention than if they were spread out to occupy the entire necklace.

Carmen Anderson
Circus Bling, 2008
0.7 x 63.5 x 2.5 cm
Handcrafted polymer clay by artist, glass pearls, rivolis, beading thread, wire; herringbone stitch, embellished buna cord
PHOTO BY ROBERT DIAMANTE

Group Together a Focal Point
This bracelet is already unified by color, stitch, and beads of uniform size. The proximity of elements grouped together in the center forms a focal point.

Melissa Ingram
Magic Carpet Ride Cuff, 2011
21 x 5 x 1 cm
Seed beads, vintage crystals, crystal pearls, polyethylene; herringbone and peyote stitch, right angle weave
PHOTO BY TWK STUDIOS

Continuation & Closure

Continuation and closure are concepts closely related. The mind continues and completes suggestions it is given. In a movie, when the scene changes from night to morning, we quite naturally fill in the missing information: night has passed, the characters slept, and we're now waking up to the next day. Similarly, when we read a story, every detail doesn't have to be supplied for our mind to furnish the gaps in the narrative with details that make sense. In our constant quest for meaning, our mind and imagination seek to unify events, objects, ideas—whatever they can—to deepen our understanding of the world.

When you arrange elements to lead the eye on a path, you're unifying them through continuation (figure 1-17). The simplest example is a single strand of beads: the beads are arranged in a continuous curve and your eye naturally follows that curve. When you line up beads (or cabochons, or any element) in a row or curve, you are creating continuation in a composition.

Continuation can take several forms:

• Patterns with good continuation may suggest that the pattern continues beyond the end of the pattern itself. Our eye has been led on a path and we mentally fill in the rest of the path (figure 1-18).

• Lining up the edges of shapes or elements is a form of continuation which unifies the elements (figure 1-19). Magazine and book layouts use continuation when they line up the edges of copy, headlines, and photos.

• Continuation is even more intriguing when not literally stated, but implied, such as in Jamie Cloud Eakin's *Cosmic Party Bracelet* (figure 1-20). Even though the line of beads is interrupted by a central cluster of cabs, your eye continues to follow it all the way to the end of the bracelet. Implied continuation actively engages viewers as they fill in the gaps.

Figure 1-17

In these three simple examples, no two beads are alike. Yet there is unity within each frame because of continuation, closure, or both.

In the frame to the right, the eye sees the beads as a curved line: they are unified by continuation.

Figure 1-18

Continuation and closure at work. A complete diagonal line is implied, even though space interrupts that line. The eye completes the line. Both continuation and closure provide unity to these randomly chosen beads.

Figure 1-19

The edges of the beads are aligned to lead the viewer on a diagonal path.

Figure 1-20   Unity and viewer involvement through continuation: you can visually follow a line from one end of the piece to the other. Even though the line is interrupted in the center of the bracelet, the fact that it appears just to the right of that center cluster implies continuation.

Jamie Cloud Eakin
Cosmic Party Bracelet, 2011
19.6 x 6.3 x 0.6 cm
Seed beads, cylinder beads, mother-of-pearl, cat's-eye glass, gold; bead embroidery
PHOTO BY STEWART O'SHIELDS

Closure is very much like implied continuation—the eye completes, or closes, an implied object.

Whenever possible, people tend to perceive a set of individual elements as a single, recognizable pattern. They will fill in missing information to complete a pattern. In figure 1-18 your eye completes the diagonal line the beads suggest. In Yvonne Baughman's *Garden of Pearls* bracelet (figure 1-21), the eye arches over the focal point to continue and close the snaking white line of beads.

Related to the concepts of continuation and closure is the repetition of direction, as in *Olivia* (page 22). As our eye follows the direction of the leaves, it continues around the circle, even when the leaves are no longer present.

Figure 1-21   Continuation draws your attention to the center. The snakelike lines use continuation to form a support and imply an arch over the central focal point. Color and repetition of beads unify the whole bracelet.

Yvonne Baughman
Garden of Pearls, 2011
19 x 8.5 x 3 cm
Crystal pearls, bicones, seed beads, linen canvas, batting, Utrasuede; bead embroidery
PHOTO BY SCOTT VAN OSDOL

**Repitition of direction is
related to continuation**
The leaves imply continuation
because they all point in the
same direction, compelling
your eye to circle the piece.

Maggie Meister
Olivia, 2010
15.2 x 19.1 x 1.3 cm
Seed beads, freshwater pearls;
right angle weave, peyote stitch
PHOTO BY GEORGE POST

Continuation and Closure
Continuation and closure are at play
in the top and bottom curved shapes.
Though they are interrupted by the
central vertical band, we see them
each as one moving element that has
descended and turned right.

Margie Deeb
Woven by Frieda Bates
Emerging Resonance, 2004
53.5 x 10.8 x 0.7 cm
Seed beads, faceted bugle and glass beads;
loom beadweaving
PHOTO BY NEIL MOORE

Emerging Patterns When you look for longer than a few seconds at a random mix of elements you'll begin to find patterns. This is continuation in action. Your eye spots areas of high contrast first: either lightest or darkest beads placed in proximity to each other. Our eye wants us to see order, thus it causes us to see lines. The lines I see are in the image on the bottom.

PATTERNS IN THE RANDOM

Sometimes we want to design something that looks as if the elements are randomly placed. This is never as easy as it seems. The eye looks for—and often finds— patterns when none are intended because of proximity, closure, and continuation. When you want a smattering of elements to look random, you need to plan carefully. Constantly scan for areas where the eye may find unintentional lines and patterns. Then deliberately interrupt them.

In the movie *The Hobbit: An Unexpected Journey*, Bilbo's dressing gown is a patchwork of colored squares. Costume designer Ann Maskrey had to carefully map out their placement so that matching blocks or blocks of similar color wouldn't be positioned next to each other and distract the viewer.

When you're designing something to appear random, it helps to have other people look at it. Ask them what they see. It's difficult to see the effects of proximity and continuation when you're the designer because you've been focused on your piece for a long time. You have a different perspective and are more likely to see what you think you see rather than what is actually visible.

The fun of continuation and closure is that they require the viewer to become more actively involved in the piece. The viewer becomes part of the art, and it is still being created, though you completed your contribution long ago. When you want to engage people more, suggest patterns or directions that the viewer must visually complete.

UNITY WITHIN SETS OF JEWELRY

All this talk of unity brings up an important issue in jewelry design: matching sets. How much do you match within a set? I posed the question to designers and received a slew of very strong opinions, all against "matchy-matchy."

Cindy Newman says, "When designing a necklace, I'm always wanting a pair of earrings to wear with it. So my challenge is how to design unique earrings that are not too matchy-matchy, but still go with."

The phrase "matchy-matchy" began in interior and fashion design and refers to a situation where all of the pieces in a room or on a person are excruciatingly alike. For example, a living room in which every pillow, cushion, rug, wall, and curtain sports the same wedgewood blue with a white polka dotted pattern.

Figure 1-22   Matchy-matchy plastic jewelry, produced by an unknown manufacturer in the 1960s, leaves little in the way of visual intrigue.

Figure 1-23   Two different approaches to matching earrings to a necklace.

Frieda Bates
Hummingbird Dreams, 2012

Necklace:
28 x 21 x 1.5 cm
Circular earrings:
8 x 3 x 1 cm
Drop earrings:
7 x 1.3 x 1 cm

Pewter, seed beads, red creek jasper, freshwater pearls, acrylic, crystals, glass pearls, polyethylene; bead embroidery with branch tassles and loops

Figure 1-24

Margo Field
Fan Dance, 2012
Necklace: 25 x 15 x 2 cm
Earrings: 5 x 4 x 1.8 cm
Seed beads, glass pearls,
pewter beads, Czech glass
beads, silver, polyethylene;
herringbone stitch, original
techniques

When several pieces of jewelry in a set look exactly alike, there can be a cheap look to it, a tacky quality. Plastic baubles from the '60s come to mind (figure 1-22). Slightly altering each piece is more intriguing to the eye, making the set fun and unique. When the earrings don't include all the colors of the necklace, or the bracelet has only half the elements the necklace features, we are drawn in to look closer.

Shared color is the main ingredient necessary for matching jewelry within sets. Sometimes, if the basic design of a necklace is simple and clean, you may not need to match stitch, design, or theme: earrings made only of the same color may be the perfect solution.

On the other hand, colors that are slightly unmatched can present an intriguing solution. For example, using blue in the earrings that is slightly darker than that used in the necklace and bracelet can add depth to the set. If you're going to alter color like this, other elements must be an exact match.

Figure 1-25

Margo Field
Seed Bead Weeds, 2012
Necklace: 25 x 15 x 2 cm
Earrings: 7 x 3 x 1.8 cm
Seed beads, glass pearls,
brass, polyethylene;
herringbone stitch, original
techniques

The goal is to have the pieces connect: create unity among them so that it's obvious they belong together. Push your imagination to find creative ways to connect the pieces without mirroring them (figures 1-23, 1-24, 1-25).

꙳

When you challenge yourself to create a striking, meticulous balance of variety and uniformity, you'll find yourself looking for new approaches, different paths. Your work will become more whole and more harmonious. And you'll achieve your style of unity.

The Ugly Necklace Contest

What happens when you deliberately avoid unity? Can you achieve ugly? Each year Warren S. Feld, owner of the Land of Odds bead store, holds The Ugly Necklace Contest. Warren has contributed greatly to beaded jewelry design with this competition, for there is much to be learned from jewelry born of the attempt and the interpretation of "ugly."

Mediocre is easy to achieve. We all can do it when we feel lazy and uninspired or we're not using our intuition or challenging ourselves. Mediocre falls in the middle of the spectrum between beautiful and ugly. Both beauty and ugliness encompass what this book is about: the deliberate application—or lack of application—of design theories. Surprisingly, like beauty, ugly isn't as easy to achieve as you might think.

On his website (www.LandofOdds.com) Warren writes, "Our eye and brain compensate for perceived imbalances: they try to correct and harmonize them. We are wired to avoid the disorienting, disturbing, or distracting. Thus it's easier to design jewelry that is inoffensive rather than downright revolting. Ugly goes against our nature. It's hard to do.

To achieve a truly hideous result requires making choices we're unfamiliar with. It takes us inside ourselves to places we usually avoid. We have to ask questions such as:
- Can I design something I do not personally like and am unwilling to wear?
- Can I create a piece of jewelry that represents a painful emotion or experience I'd prefer to avoid?
- Can I make something I know others won't like and may ridicule me for?"

Warren continues his discussion of ugly: "Jewelry designers who attempt to achieve 'Ugly' for this contest have to exert control and discipline to override intuitive, internally integrated principles of artistic beauty. We've found that the

Warren writes, "This piece fails to sustain a satisfying rhythm. No pattern is established, and there are no points of interest to motivate the viewer to want to see the whole piece from end to end."

No kidding, Warren!

Nivya Raju
Untitled, 2008
81 x 61 x 26 cm
Glass and plastic beads, metal, memory wire, foam, steel wool, nylon, badminton shuttlecocks; stringing, wire wrapping

best jewelry designers are those who can prove that they can design a truly ugly necklace."

One thing I found interesting was that entries that focused more on the ridiculous were not necessarily ugly. While they were over-the-top in their absurdity and far from beautiful, I wouldn't consider them ugly. Ugly must consciously defy sound design principles.

Lynn Margaret Davy
Untitled, 2008
72 x 38 x 9 cm
Glass and plastic beads,
metal, wire, feather,
rubber, string, velvet,
foil, ceramic; peyote
stitch, stringing, wire
wrapping, brick stitch

Corrine Zephier
Untitled, 2008
76 x 51 x 15 cm
Glass and plastic beads, metal, wire, wood, insects,
plastic, brass, string, fabric; peyote stitch, stringing,
daisy chain, brick stitch

The critera for judging includes:
- lack of balance
- lack of focus
- lack of movement and bad rhythm
- violation of color principles
- disorientation (no sense of top or bottom)
- wearability (piece must be wearable and as
  ugly or uglier when worn)
- overall hideousness
- parsimony

Warren describes parsimony as "the degree the
piece is over- or underdone. For example, one
entry used over 20 plastic trolls while less would
have made the point and been uglier. Repeating
the same ugly component doesn't necessarily
result in an uglier necklace. In fact, the repetition
led to more unity."

What do all the entries pictured here share? Lack
of unity: not enough repetition for cohesiveness,
too much variety, no regard for proximity, no
continuation or closure. Examine them and you'll
find the rest of the design principles outlined in
this book have been deviated from or ignored. We
bestow the title of "ugly" upon them because of
their flagrant lack of unity.

Unity Study

CAROL DEAN SHARPE AND I explored unity by changing degrees of variety in her *Ribbed Cuff Peyote Bracelet*. The purpose is not to declare one level better than the other, but rather to explore how variety affects unity.

When made with only size 11° seed beads, the bracelet resembles a solid piece of fabric with textural ribs. Its design is conservative, refined, and understated, affording ample room for variety.

As embellishments are added, variety is introduced, a little more in each consecutive version.

How do the variations affect the unity of the design?

1 This version is constructed of the same seed beads throughout.

2 Metallic bronze beads form each rib, adding a hint of variety in the bead finish and color.

3 The introduction of large faceted beads creates size and texture variation.

4 Color, size, texture, and bead finish variation create a lively piece of jewelry that retains harmonious unity.

Carol Dean Sharpe
Ribbed Cuff Peyote Bracelet, 2012
3.8 x 24.5 x 0.5 cm
Cylinder beads; peyote stitch

Challenge Yourself

1   Select two pieces of jewelry, one you consider successful and one you consider an unsuccessful design. Choose them from a book or magazine or use jewelry that you've made. Examine each for unity in each the following categories:

Repetition
- Are enough elements repeated to provide visual cohesion?
- Is there so much repetition that it is predictable and boring?

Variety
- Is there enough variety to intrigue you in each piece?

Proximity
- How are the elements positioned within the piece of jewelry?
- Are the elements clustered so as to guide the eye?

Continuation
- Are there enough visual clues to compel the eye to move effortlessly through the piece?

What principle of unity does each piece emphasize? What does it lack?

In your estimation, where does each piece land on the Unitometer? Do you find any correlation with its position on the Unitometer and its level of success?

2   Design two pair of earrings, each pair emphasizing one of these four principles of unity: repetition, variety, proximity, continuation.

3   As a designer, what would you do to a strand of pearls to give it more variety while maintaining unity?

4   Imagine you are given a 4-pound bag of beads in countless shapes, sizes, textures, and colors. How would you plan a piece of jewelry from these beads? What choices would you make? Where would you begin to fashion unity out of this randomness?

2 | Focal Point & Emphasis

Our task as designers is to guide viewers into the world of our jewelry. I like to imagine my pieces beckoning with extended hand: "Look, dear traveler, here is where you start: at the heart of the matter. Let me tell you a story of the beauty, wonder, and fascination I've known with these colors, these shapes, these beads, this light. Now, shift your focus here, to the left ... see?"

The way to guide viewers is through carefully planned focal points and emphasis, as other artists do.

Musicians guide their listeners through a composition using calculated harmonies, dissonance, and eventual resolution. Writers guide their readers through a story, carefully crafting what the reader will hear, see, and experience. Painters invite their viewers into the painting at a specific point on the canvas and direct the eye to keep exploring within the scene.

Our goal is to first attract the eye, then guide it. We consciously design an entry point and a subsequent path for the eye to travel. Let's discuss some of the most powerful ways to do this.

Figure 2-1   Areas of high value and color contrast, like the bright earring, capture attention.

Margie Deeb
Woven by Frieda Bates
The Golden Earring, 2003
Seed, cylinder, and pressed glass beads; loom beadweaving
19.1 x 11.4 x 0.5 cm
PHOTO BY HAIGWOOD STUDIOS

Figure 2-2

Margie Deeb
Loom work by Frieda Bates
Mandira, 2003
20.3 x 10.2 x 0.5 cm
Cylinder beads, amethyst
drop, vermeil clasp; loom
beadweaving, braiding

CONTRAST, THE GREAT ATTRACTOR

Our eye is captivated by contrast; it makes a beeline
to dissimilarity. When an element within a piece
of jewelry contrasts with the prevailing design, it
becomes the focal point. Attract attention in your
design by contrasting the following elements:

Value Contrast

Value refers to how dark or light a color is. The
effect that strategic arrangement of lights and darks
has on composition is potent. When a small light
area is displayed on a large dark background it grabs
attention. A small dark spot on a light background
does the same. In *The Golden Earring* (figure 2-1), the
bright earring is the area of highest contrast, both in
value and color. It demands your attention first. Your
focus then slides left and up to the profile emerging
from the shadows. I carefully arranged value contrast
in *Mandira* (figures 2-2 through 2-4) to pull viewers
in and keep their attention circling back to the face.

Figure 2-3   The largest, lightest area—the
left side of the face—contains the
area of highest contrast: dark eye
and brow. By arranging contrast
I consciously guide the viewer's
attention here first.

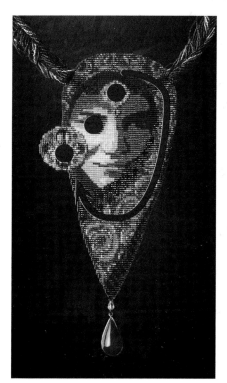

Figure 2-4   The whole piece contains a well
defined path: the viewer follows
three calculated points of interest
diagonally up and right, then
circles back around the lightest
area of the scarf, and back to the
large medallion. Eyes are a natural
focal point in portraiture.

Shape Contrast

Circles or curved shapes attract attention when contrasted against geometric shapes and straight edges. Likewise, lines and angles become the focal point when surrounded by curves (figure 2-5).

Pattern, Texture & Density Contrast

A small, highly textured or patterned area within a smooth expanse draws immediate attention. Conversely, so will a small smooth area on a highly textured or patterned background (figure 2-6).

Size Contrast

One large element surrounded by smaller elements stands out; a cluster of small elements surrounded by larger ones can draw the most attention (figure 2-7).

Color Contrast

Colors that contrast rivet attention. Black and white advertisements in which the product is the only spot of color are the most obvious example of using color contrast as a focal point to attract the eye. The bracelet in figure 2-7 keeps your eye moving within the center by contrasting not only size, but also color. Bold red seizes attention when surrounded by softer blues, greens, and grays. Attract the eye more subtly by placing a splash of the complementary color among analogous colors (explained on page 99), like *The Golden Earring* (figure 2-1), which uses the complementary harmony (see page 100) of purple and yellow.

When designing your next necklace, do you want viewers to enter at the front and center? Or would you rather they enter just off to the side, then meander to the center? Do you want the viewer looking at a pair of earrings to focus solidly on them, or would you rather have their gaze start at the earrings, then shift to the wearer's face? Consciously decide and position your contrasts—especially color contrasts—accordingly, for they are entry points into the piece.

Figure 2-5

The geometric shape and ordered pattern of the focal bead strongly contrasts against the curved and irregular shaped beads surrounding it.

Sherry Duquet
Ocean Reflection, 2009
Dimensions unknown
Turquoise, sterling silver; stringing
PHOTO BY STEWART O'SHIELDS

Figure 2-6

The contrast of a uniformly stitched area surrounding an intricate frontispiece acts as a frame, drawing focus to the center. The busy fringe and strap continue the interplay of pattern and texture contrast.

Rebecca Starry
Twisted, 2009
33 x 17.8 x 2.5 cm
Seed beads, drill bits, chuck keys, chain and assorted findings, beading thread; right angle weave, twisted fringe and assorted offloom stitches
PHOTO BY JESSICA STEPHENS

Figure 2-7

Andrea L. Stern
Temple Gate Bracelet, 2009
Dimensions unknown
Coral, Chinese porcelain, glass beads, Thai silver; stringing, wirework
PHOTO BY STEWART O'SHIELDS

THE VISUAL PATH

Now that you've attracted your viewer's attention, you want the eyes to stay within the piece, exploring. You want them to walk a visual path. For this to happen, you must consciously design that path.

When we look at something, our eye naturally stops and lingers at the points of focus. As explained earlier, these areas are the points of contrast. Our attention is captured wherever we see something different, something that stands out from its surroundings. Often you'll want to design secondary points of interest (more subtle than the main focal point) and to connect them with a visual path. That path can be obvious (figure 2-8) or subtle (figure 2-9).

Curves, lines, or shapes that direct the eye inward keep the attention dancing within the piece of jewelry. Avoid elements that point out and away from the piece unless you've created counterbalancing elements that guide the eye back into the piece (figures 2-10 and 2-11).

When a stage magician needs to distract the audience, say with a coin, he moves it in an arc. The curving action temporarily confuses those observing so he can perform an illusion. On the other hand, if the magician moves the coin in a straight line, the viewer's eyes spring back like an elastic band to the origin of the move.

Curves manage the movements of viewers' eyes by keeping them within the composition. In addition to creating a more voluptuous and appealing design, the curve is the most effective device for leading the eye to focal points.

Look at a piece of jewelry you've designed that features a focal point. Is there a visual path made of secondary points of interest? If so, how obvious or subtle is the path? If not, do you think a visual path would enhance the piece? Are curves used to help define the path?

Figure 2-8

Your eyes are pulled around the stone and down to the bottom of the fringe by curving lines with dark accents.

Derralynne McMaster
Pink Peruvian Opal Slab Necklace, 2008
45 x 20 x 11 cm
Pink Peruvian opal, picasso jasper, sterling silver; micro macrame, peyote stitch

Figure 2-9

The eye tends to make paths that connect the same or similar colors. When I look at this, I immediately see a blue path beginning at the bottom left leading me up and ending at the top left. A secondary path connects the area of the lightest color, the yellow greens.

Jamie Cloud Eakin
Playin' with Paisley, 2011
Focal section:
31.8 x 12 x 3 cm
Rivolis, crystals, seed beads; bead embroidery
PHOTO BY ARTIST

Figure 2-10

Even though the three flowers are similar, the center blossom is the focal point because of its central position. It is there that our eyes enter, circle around the leaves, then sweep up the sides of the necklace following the direction of the small leaves. With their substance and presence, the flowers endlessly compel the eye back to the center front.

Margo Field
Silica Lace, 2012
Focal section: 28 x 18 x 2 cm
Seed beads, glass pearls, brass; peyote stitch, netting, original techniques

To Center or Not to Center?

The most common position for a focal point is the center. Symmetrical compositions with a focal point at the center are easier to design, and easy to read visually. They create a stable, orderly composition. Because our bodies are visually symmetrical and our faces feature a central focal point (the nose), centered focal points are perfectly suited to jewelry, especially necklaces.

When all elements on a necklace are similar, we naturally gravitate first to the center. In Margo Fields' necklace (figure 2-10), the position of the central flower creates a focal point, even though it is flanked by two identical ones.

As natural as they are, sometimes symmetrical compositions with a central focal point can be so static they become uninteresting. Maybe you've made one that seems to just "sit there" saying nothing, putting you to sleep. If this is the case, try positioning the main focal point off-center.

Off-center focal points are more dynamic than centered ones because the visual weight is not equally distributed. But be careful: When your focal point is off-center you run the risk of lopsidedness. You must counterbalance the visual weight of the focal point (we'll talk about this in Chapter 3, Balance). And you'll need to avoid placing the focal point so close to an edge that it leads the viewer's eye out of the jewelry.

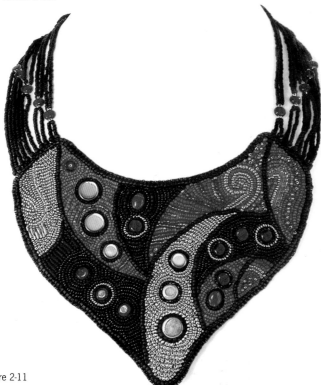

Figure 2-11

I deliberately designed the curved shapes and lines to keep your eye circling endlessly within the boundaries of the necklace. Notice the shape is symmetrical while the composition within it is not.

Margie Deeb
Untitled, 2008
Focal section: 24 x 24 x 1 cm
Cylinder beads, Czech glass; bead embroidery

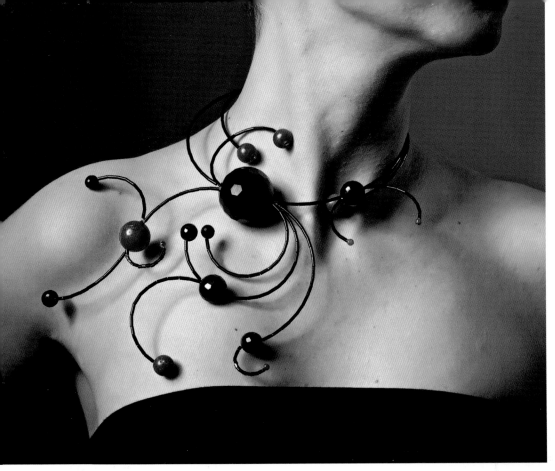

Lead 'em back to the focal point
Curving pathways effortlessly direct our eye to the large black bead. The semicircle embracing the shoulder could provide an exit, however it is counterbalanced by all the activity surrounding the focal point.

Julia Dusman
Tarantula, 2010
23 x 20 x 2 cm
Black onyx, sponge coral, carnelian, glass, wire
PHOTO BY JENS LOOK

Consciously guide the eye around and back into the composition
An implied gentle S-curve (from the top left sprig of hair down to the point of the beak at the bottom) guides the eye down while the egg shape coaxes it around and back into the focal point. Fascinating life forms, activity, texture, and color keep our attention riveted to the center.

Judie Mountain and Wayne Robbins
Serendipity, 2010
70 cm long
Torchworked glass, Czech glass, copper metal clay, branch pearls, brass, horse hair; sculpted, hand formed
PHOTO BY PAUL SCHRAUB

Figure 2-12

The strength of this design lies in the overall interplay of intriguing elements, pattern, rhythm, and structure.

Marcia DeCoster
En Pointe, 2011
14 x 24 x 0.5 cm
Seed beads; right angle weave
PHOTO BY ARTIST

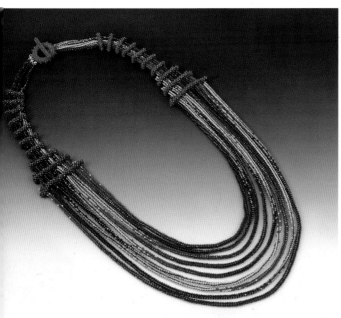

Figure 2-13

The intriguing color gradations of each strand keep us within the piece.

Rachel Nelson-Smith
Dive, 2011
51 x 51 x 6 cm
Seed beads, nylon, silver; tubular 1-drop peyote stitch, flat 1-drop right angle weave, wirework
PHOTO BY ARTIST

Figure 2-14

Joanna Gollberg
Turquoise Bead Choker, 2006
Neckwire: 40.6 cm long
Dangles: 2.5 to 6.4 cm
Turquoise beads, silver; wirework, stringing
PHOTO BY JOHN WIDMAN

WHOLE-OVER-THE-PARTS EMPHASIS

Rather than a single focal point, an overall feature, like pattern or structure, can be the point of focus. This is referred to as *whole-over-the-parts emphasis*. Seed bead weaving whose overall texture forms the main visual interest fall into this category.

Each element is the same in Marcia DeCoster's necklace, *En Point* (figure 2-12). Although the front and center is slightly modulated, it is not a focal point. The visual emphasis is the whole necklace. Within each element, contrast captures our attention: color contrast, structural contrast, and the contrast of woven beads and open space. But it is the necklace as a whole we focus on, looking back and forth from element to element, visually unraveling the intricate, puzzle-like pieces interlocking to form a beautiful necklace.

Like a flamboyant tropical bird, Rachel Nelson-Smith's necklace (figure 2-13) attracts us with vibrant color gradations. In Joanna Gollberg's necklace (figure 2-14) your eyes delight in tracking the alternating positions of the turquoise beads. Both necklaces invite us to revel in the overall piece as each element affirms its connection with the rest through their inspired whole-over-the-parts approach to unity.

Allover Pattern

When the emphasis is the pattern of an entire piece, rather than a specific focal point, *allover pattern* becomes the focus. Most often, allover pattern features consistently repeated elements, like that of traditional upholstery fabric or quilts. Repeated elements in traditional bargello create a geometric allover pattern (figure 2-15).

Some of the most alluring allover patterns are not made of precisely repeating elements. Irregular sizing of the same or similar elements creates variety within the unity. Representational illustrations such as tattoos feature patterns made of non-repeating elements that share similar color, motif, and line style (figure 2-16).

SPACE

In design, space is defined by its surrounding elements and is as important as those elements. When handled consciously and creatively, space becomes an entirely new visual element, as it does in Patricia Zabreski Venaleck's necklace (figure 2-17).

In jewelry, space can either be an absence of elements, or holes cut out of elements (figures 2-18 through 2-20). Space can also refer to areas less busy, less laden with embellishment and visual intricacy. I equate designing this kind of "quiet space" into a piece with placing a bench in a garden. The bench affords the viewer space to pause, reflect, and revel in the beauty.

Figure 2-15

Ann Benson
Castle Tapestry Bag, 2010
5 x 6.5 x 0.5 cm
Seed beads; bead crochet
PHOTO BY STEWART O'SHIELDS

Allover pattern

iStockPhoto/Elixirpix

Figure 2-16

Margie Deeb
Henna Tattoo Earrings, 2012
4.7 x 3.5 x 0.5 cm
Basswood, copper, ink, acrylic; painting, wood work, wire work

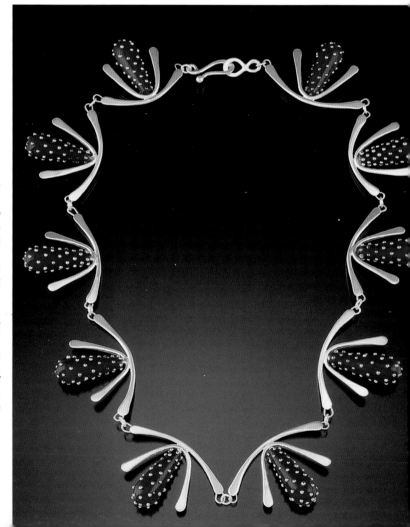

Figure 2-17

The spaces created by the "wings" that frame each patterned bead become an element, contributing to the beautiful, undulating rhythym.

Patricia Zabreski Venaleck
Fire, 2012
Bead size:
0.4 x 2.4 x 2.7 cm
Handmade lampwork beads and forged/soldered silver wire
PHOTO BY LARRY SANDERS

Figures 2-18, 2-19, 2-20

SaraBeth Cullinan
Cleopatra, 2000
50.8 x 5.5 cm
Seed beads, glass cabochon, Czech
pressed glass; herringbone, peyote, and
square stitch, bead embroidery, stringing

Candace Cloud McLean
Evening Air, 2009
43 x 5 x 0.7 cm
Cane glass beads, glass pearls,
crystals, stainless steel;
wirework and stringing

SaraBeth Cullinan
Amari, 2008
50.8 x 5 cm
Rhodonite, 14k gold-filled beads, crystals;
stringing, square stitch

Figure 2-18   Figure 2-19   Figure 2-20

Empty space is referred to as *negative space,* because nothing occupies it. In the case of jewelry, the skin or fabric underneath fills that space, so it's not actually empty. The magic of skin peeking through sparkling color and metal can be that of the enchantress or the seductress.

Space is as important as beads in defining the shape, weight, and visual impact of jewelry. Just as you consciously shape the elements you weave together, you need to consciously shape negative space. Approach space as the visual element it is.

When creating multistrand necklaces, the proportion of space between strands to the strand width and curve is very important. If the strands are different lengths, you'll want the space between the strands to be regular and even, as in SaraBeth Cullinan's necklace (figure 2-21).

Space lightens visual weight. If every section of the bracelet in figure 2-22 had been a solid disc rather than an open ring, the bracelet would appear much heavier.

Remember, with or without a focal point, your goal is to guide the viewer's eye into the piece and keep it there, lingering and exploring. With no focal point, you need to pay even more attention to the overall pattern, texture, structure, and color of each element. Focus on integrating all of the elements into a beautiful, enduring whole.

Figure 2-21   **SaraBeth Cullinan**
Lavender Morning, 2009
48 cm long
Freshwater pearls, gold-filled and vermeil beads,
glass crystals and pearls, faceted amethyst,
lampworked beads; stringing

Figure 2-22   Space plays an important compositional role here: every other disc is bisected, altering its shape.

SaraBeth Cullinan
Spring Bracelet, 2011
19 x 2 cm
Seed beads, cylinder beads, crystals; peyote stitch, surface embellishment

Figure 2-23

Gretchen Coats
Crystal Lilac, 2012
30 x 10 x 2.7 cm
Seed beads, Czech and Chinese
crystal, amethyst; right angle
weave, chevron chain stitch, netting

MYSTERY

When it comes to making vivid and compelling art, I'll share a secret I've discovered: Imbue the piece with mystery.

Unfortunately, instructions for the deliberate creation of mystery are impossible. I can, however, describe our reactions to it...and our reactions hold valuable clues.

In Mystery's Presence

You can feel the presence of mystery. You sense a sacredness. You gaze at a piece of jewelry and your mind leaps. You feel awe. You feel wonder. You want to figure out why you're so drawn to it, and you're inspired to make something as exciting or beautiful. In the presence of mystery you feel more alive and empowered as an artist.

Look at a piece of jewelry that stops you in your tracks, one you can't stop thinking about, or one you wish you had created. Can you sense the mystery in it? Can you feel yourself drawn in, seduced as if by a magical spell? I feel this when I look at much of Heidi Kummli's work. The mystery she creates is both within and beyond the intricacies and drama of her work.

Mystery can lie in the simplest design. Think of Georgia O'Keeffe's paintings: swaths of color and shapes pared down to their essence. Gretchen Coats' *Crystal Lilac* necklace (figure 2-23) captivates me, because

I sense a depth in its simplicity, as if much more exists here than I can see. It calls to me yet I can't put words to what I hear. I'm surprised and delighted by designs so elegantly uncomplicated. They mesmerize me.

The materials, texture, and positioning of elements in *Mad Hatter* (figure 2-24) intrigue me. Yet something deeper is brewing within those tangibles. They conspire to lure me in, and the longer I look, the deeper I'm drawn into their enchantment. I'm spellbound. It's hard for me to break my gaze.

Creating mystery in your art can't be listed in steps; it transcends the straitjacket of language. The process itself is mysterious. Clues can be found, however, in the effects it has on those touched by it. My advice: Steep yourself in the effects of mystery while you create. Feel the wonder, be inspired, be excited. Let your passion fuel you. Be awed by the beauty, color, light, or form of your materials. Be enchanted by the process of creativity. This will imbue your work with a touch of mystery.

If you determine the entry point of your piece, prioritize and order the contrast and thus the composition, allow space for lingering, and impart a touch of mystery, you will create stunning jewelry.

Figure 2-24

Heidi Kummli and Sherry Serafini
Mad Hatter, 2011
25.5 x 15 x 1.3 cm
Seed beads, glass and natural cabochons,
beetle wings, bone; bead embroidery
PHOTO BY HEIDI KUMMLI

Focal Point Study

AS STATED EARLIER, the designer's task is to guide the viewer's eye. We begin by consciously creating a focal point, an area of interest. We then construct a visual path made by secondary focal points in a hierarchical manner.

Focal points can be:

• the brightest areas (most luminous colors)

• the lightest areas

• the darkest areas

• areas of concentrated value contrast (lightest against darkest, or vice versa)

• texture against smooth background, or vice versa

• a large bead among many small beads, or vice versa

Version 1

In these earrings I explored how the positioning of color—specifically lights and darks—guides the eye. The two versions differ only in arrangement of color.

Can you find the focal point in Version #1? There are several:

• the eye is drawn across the horizontal band created by the lightest beads (not an aesthetically pleasing focal point)

• the upper medallion section seems a natural focal point because of the circular shape, but the horizontal band competes with it, causing visual confusion

• the horizontal band cuts the earring horizontally and fights with the vertical draping of the three loops, diminishing the elegance of the composition

Version 2

Version #2 resolves the problems in Version #1:

• the eye is drawn immediately into the upper center where the lightest beads are located

• the upper center is a structural focal point because it is a circular center, thus composition and color are in agreement

Second Focal Point

• the eye shifts from the medallion straight down the earring to a second focal point—the six large silver beads

• the second focal point is a recognizable triangle shape which augments the length and drape, making an elegant composition

• this is a much stronger design because the viewer's eye is guided on a vertical path

Margie Deeb
Mini-Radiant Sun Earings, 2008
5.5 x 3.3 x 0.7 cm
Faceted Czech glass beads, seed beads; right angle weave, stringing

Challenge Yourself

1 **Focal Point & Guiding the Eye** Visit an online gallery of jewelry where you can view several thumbnail-sized images simultaneously. You want to look at thumbnails (images less than 3 inches [7.6 cm]) because it's easier to follow the visual path when seeing smaller images. Be conscious of how your eye scans each piece. Where does it enter the piece? Does it move about within the piece or move quickly out? If it stays within, why? What compels your eye to move certain ways?

2 **Focal Point** Choose three pieces you've made and examine them by asking:

- Are there areas of contrast? If so, what kind of contrast: value, pattern, density, shape, size, color?
- Is there a focal point or whole-over-the-parts emphasis?
- If there is a focal point, is it centered or off-centered?
- Is there a clear visual path for the eye to follow?

3 **Space** Consciously design a piece of jewelry that incorporates negative space as an element. You may weave several components such as rings or other open shapes. Be as aware of and deliberate with the shapes you create using space as you are of the shapes you create with physical elements.

4 **Allover Pattern** Design a pair of earrings using a very simple geometric shape, such as a circle or square. Focus on making an intriguing allover pattern within that shape. Remember, your pattern can be made of elements that are all uniform in size, or different sizes.

5 **Mystery** Cultivate a passion for mystery. For example, I'm enchanted by lemurs. I'm entranced by their beauty, their grace, and their mystery. I have questions about them that can never be answered. I frequently set aside time to learn about and ponder lemurs. When I do this my spirit is lifted and expanded. It may sound odd, but it opens my imagination and creativity in ways nothing else can.

Keep a journal or a digital doc where you jot down what makes your heart and mind surge with wonder. What makes you feel more alive and empowered? What inspires you to make something as exciting, challenging, or beautiful? Cultivate these emotions, for they are more powerful than you can imagine. When you design your next piece, tap into that resonance. Consciously take a moment before beginning your work session and feel it. Let the feelings weave their way through your heart, mind, hands, and your work as you create.

3 | Balance

Balance is an integral part of our lives. As long as gravity remains a force, we'll need balance. If you've traveled by boat or ridden a bicycle, you know how critical balance is to your body and well-being.

We all possess an innate sense of balance. When something is visually off-balance, we feel it—it disturbs us. We don't want to feel off-balance. Nor do we want to look lopsided when adorned with our beaded creations. So let's explore ways to achieve visual balance, both symmetrical and asymmetrical. Balance takes us a step further in achieving the unity we seek in jewelry design.

The strung necklace by Jamie Cloud Eakin in figure 3-1 demonstrates balance in several ways. At first glance it appears a relatively simple, strung necklace. Look longer and you see the careful planning involved in creating exquisite visual balance. Thoughtful use of materials, their presence, placement, and spacing, is just the beginning.

Figure 3-1 This necklace is a beautiful example of balance in every way. Textural contrast is balanced between metal and glass, and shiny and matte surfaces. Explore the balance in composition and movement on the next page.

Jamie Cloud Eakin
Pearl Parade, 2009
45 x 20.3 x 1.5 cm
Mother-of-pearl, freshwater pearls, lampwork glass, chain, wire, seed beads; wire-work, stringing

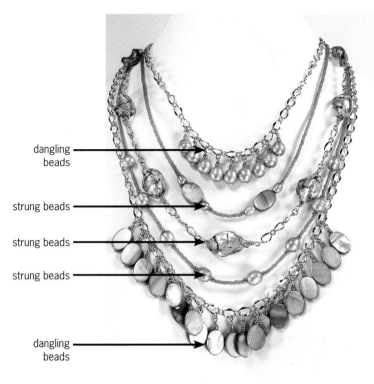

Balance of Composition Placement of each major bead or grouping of beads is carefully controlled to accomplish equilibrium. A unified whole is created by all five strands sharing the spotlight: No strand competes with the other.

Balance of Movement Visual and kinetic variety is achieved by the beads being attached differently—some strung, some hung. These hanging techniques are deliberately balanced: beads dangle from top and bottom strands, while the center 3 strands feature strung beads.

strand width is 5% of pendant width

strand width is 10% of pendant width

strand width is 15% of pendant width

strand width is 20% of pendant width

Balancing Strap-to-Pendant Proportions

Which proportion do you prefer?

Ideally, seeing the colors and materials would help you make the best choice.

If the pendant is dark and solid, it will be visually heavier. Therefore, it will require a thicker strand.

If the pendant is made of loosely wrapped wire and appears open and airy, its visual weight is quite light. A very thin strand would provide the best visual balance.

See the Visual Balance Study on page 56 for more about strap-to-pendant proportions.

SYMMETRICAL & ASYMMETRICAL BALANCE

Symmetrical balance, the kind we're most familiar with, occurs when you place and repeat similar shapes along a vertical or horizontal axis. Think mirror image. It is the easiest to create, and the one you see most often. Symmetrical balance is referred to as *formal balance*. Because it is static, demonstrating very little movement, it conveys stability and calmness.

Vertical & Horizontal Symmetry

Vertical symmetry occurs when the right and left side of the image mirror each other: the mirror image occurs on a vertical axis (figure 3-3). Butterflies and the human body display vertical symmetry.

Horizontal symmetry occurs along a horizontal axis, with the bottom half mirroring the top. Horizontal symmetry evokes a reflection, and tends to the pictorial or illustrative (figure 3-4).

The image of the human body is vertically symmetrical; the left and right sides are visually the same (figure 3-2). We are not horizontally symmetrical; the upper half of our body is different from the lower half.

Figure 3-2
The human form displays vertical symmetry: a mirror image from side to side.

Margie Deeb
Holding the Hope, 2011
41 x 9 cm
Seed beads, Lucite, glass cabochons; bead embroidery, stringing

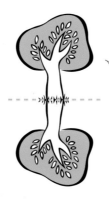

Figure 3-3

Vertical Symmetry
One side mirrors the other on a vertical axis.

Figure 3-4

Horizontal Symmetry
A tree reflected in water creates a mirror image on a horizontal axis.

Figure 3-5

Vertical and Horizontal Symmetry
The mirror image occurs from top to bottom and left to right.

Figure 3-6

Vertical and horizontal symmetry
are created by repeating the same
shapes and elements in the same
position on the left and right side,
and on the top and bottom.

Laura McCabe
Serpentine Spiked Cuff, 2010
17 x 4.5 x 2 cm
Custom-cut stones, glass seed beads, crystals, freshwater pearls,
sterling silver; tubular peyote stitch, flat peyote stitch, embellishment
PHOTO BY MELINDA HOLDEN

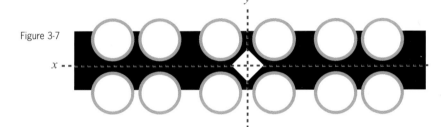

Figure 3-7

Because we are upright creatures built
on a vertical axis, most jewelry designs
are symmetrical either vertically, or
both vertically and horizontally. You
seldom see horizontal symmetry on
its own.

When both vertical and horizontal
symmetry are present, the mirror
image occurs side-to-side and top-to-
bottom, as in flowers with even petals
(figure 3-5).

Laura McCabe's *Serpentine Spiked Cuff*
(figure 3-6) displays both vertical and
horizontal symmetry. Figure 3-7 is
a diagram of the composition. See
how both the X and the Y axis are
mirrored? Laura has managed to
accomplish the unusual juxtaposition
of very formal balance within a
contemporary design.

A design can be formal and look
symmetrical without containing
precise vertical and horizontal
symmetry. Met Innmon achieves
this by repeating and overlapping
elements that point in one direction
only (figure 3-8).

Figure 3-8

Each vertically
symmetrical triangular
element is repeated,
radiating from a central
point. There is no mirror-
image, yet it is a visually
symmetrical design.

Met Innmon
Chevron On and On, 2010
25 x 5.7 x 1.3 cm
Seed beads, beading thread;
peyote and whip stitch
PHOTO BY LARRY HANSEN

Radial Balance

Snowflakes are one of our world's exquisite wonders, perfectly designed beauty falling from the sky, each one different. Snowflakes show us symmetrical radial balance: each identical spoke radiates out from a central point (figure 3-9).

Radial balance need not be symmetrical. When the central point is off center, asymmetrical radial balance occurs (figure 3-10). Betsy Youngquist has used both symmetrical and asymmetrical motifs in her intriguing *Eye Flower Pins* (figure 3-11).

ASYMMETRICAL BALANCE

Asymmetrical balance can be more interesting than symmetrical balance because it is less predictable. It allows more dynamic design and greater freedom of expression. We can't actually measure this informal balance, but we strongly sense it. We know when something is balanced or "off." We feel it. For this reason, asymmetrical balance must be more carefully planned than symmetrical balance. A simple example of informal, asymmetrical balance is figure 3-12.

There is no simple formula for achieving asymmetrical balance. The goal is to use and distribute elements that, rather than being identical, have *equal eye attraction*. You are relying on visual weight, not actual weight, to provide balance. And you are relying on your senses, not a scale or ruler, to calculate that visual weight.

Figure 3-9

Symmetrical Radial Balance
All elements radiate out from a central point.

Figure 3-10

Asymmetrical Radial Balance
The midpoint is off-center.

Figure 3-11

The petals demonstrate radial balance. The eyes display vertical symmetry.

Betsy Youngquist
Eye Flower Pins, 2009
4 x 4 x 1.3 cm
Seed beads, bugle beads, vintage glass stones, antique glass doll eyes, grout, silver-plated pewter findings, base metal pin backs; mosaic
PHOTO BY LARRY SANDERS

Figure 3-12   Left: There is no mirror image within this element, yet it is visually balanced. The activity on the top which extends to the left counterbalances the heavy weight of the leaf extending to the right.
Right: Without the left extending flourish, the motif loses balance.

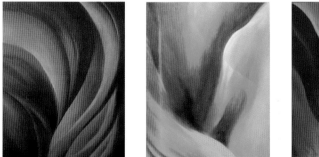

Figure 3-13   Asymmetrical balance provides compelling composition that hints at more unknown, unmeasurable, unpredictable mysteries.

Margie Deeb
Untitled, 2008
30.5 x 45.7 cm
Oil on canvas

Figure 3-14

Cynthia Deis
Barcelona, 2008
45.7 cm
Labradorite, freshwater
pearls, brass filigree;
stringing, wire wrapping
PHOTO BY STEWART O'SHIELDS

Figure 3-15

The shape is symmetrical
(mirror image) while the
design within is asymmetrical
(no mirror image). The curves
inside the main shape evoke
the dynamic grace of a spiral,
and counterbalance each
other with their opposing
directions.

Margie Deeb
Untitled, 2007
32 x 12.7 x 0.8 cm
Chrysocolla, turquoise, amethyst
chalcedony, vintage pressed
glass, 24k gold and glass beads;
bead embroidery, stringing

Figure 3-16

Both shape and design are
asymmetrical. The weight of
the intricate embroidery on
the upper left side is balanced
by the visual weight of three
strands on the right. A central
stone resolves the composition
into beautiful equilibrium.

Jamie Cloud Eakin
Turbulence, 2010
Focal element: 24 x 24.3 x 1 cm
Ruby in fuchsite, chalk turquoise,
freshwater pearl, mountain jade,
green quartz, magnesite; bead
embroidery, stringing

I'm enthralled by asymmetrical
arrangements composed of
sensual, sweeping curves and
diagonals—they're a common
motif in my art (figure 3-13). The
drama, tension, and movement
this asymmetry brews gives a
sense of mystery.

All three necklaces on this page
are asymmetrically balanced
in different ways. Cynthia Deis
uses a focal point on a necklace
that is completely different
from the left to the right side
(figure 3-14). In figure 3-15
the composition within the
bounds of a symmetrical shape
is assymetrical. Both shape and
design are asymmetrical in Jamie
Cloud Eakin's necklace
(figure 3-6).

Techniques of Asymmetrical Balance

Because of the enticing
unpredictability of asymmetrical
balance, I find myself compelled
to look longer, seeking the not-
so-obvious source of balance.
Stylish, contemporary jewelry
design (especially metalwork)
leans heavily on asymmetrical
balance, which can be achieved
in many ways. We'll explore the
following methods:

- value and color
- position
- texture and pattern
- shape
- movement

Value and Color

Darker colors, those with lower value, are visually heavier than lighter colors. You can use a larger area of a lighter color to counterbalance a small area of dark (figures 3-17 through 3-19).

Balancing dark and light is simple. When color is added, it becomes more complex. With color we need to consider luminosity—the brilliance of a color. A color's brightness affects visual weight.

A small amount of a darker or *muted* (less saturated, more dull) color can counterbalance an expanse of a lighter color (top of figure 3-20). But when luminosity comes into play we need to look more carefully. Bright, luminous colors demand more attention than colors that are simply lighter. To show you what I mean, look at the bottom of figure 3-20. This yellow is very luminous. Because its brilliance demands attention, yellow can appear to dominate the darker, muted blue. Do you sense the difference in balance between the two examples?

In figure 3-21, each side of an asymmetrical design is assigned a different proportion of two different colors. One color is darker and more muted, the other lighter and brighter. Use your innate sense of balance to determine which you feel is more balanced.

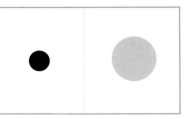

Figure 3-17

Balance through Value
The darker a color (lower value), the more visual weight it carries. A small dark element is visually equal to a lighter (higher value) larger element.

Figure 3-18

Because the smaller circle in the upper center is darker and more active with texture and detail, it balances the larger, lighter, less active one beneath it.

Gretchen Coats
Awakening, 2010
38 x 28 x 1.8 cm
Seed beads, Czech glass, fire-polished beads, rivolis, turquoise, lampworked glass, sterling wire; bead embroidery, peyote stitch

Figure 3-19

Balance through Value
Left: Because the smallest circle is dark (visually heavy) it balances all three lighter, larger circles. The positioning of lights and darks balances the composition.

Right: The dark circle in the earring balances the whole circle because its visual weight is equal to the crescent and the lightest circle.

Figure 3-20

Balance through Color
Top: The darker, less-saturated blue visually balances the larger expanse of a lighter color. The yellow is slightly muted, with a hint or orange.

Bottom: The yellow is bright and luminous, demanding more attention than the heavier blue. Do you feel a visual balance from the left to right? Does the upper example feel more balanced?

Figure 3-21

Balance through Color
On the left the darker, muted color occupies a smaller area. On the right the lighter, brighter color occupies a smaller area. Do you feel that one is more balanced than the other?

With her sure eye for equilibrium, Francine Walker has achieved balance through careful distribution of value, hue, and color intensity (figure 3-22).

Position

The goal of ikebana, the Japanese art of flower arranging, is to achieve exquisite asymmetrical balance. This is most often accomplished through position. The artist will place more materials on one side to balance a single, spectacular flower on the other. Such asymmetrical balance creates rhythm, movement, and a defined visual path. Ikebana arrangements look deceptively simple. Mastery of this art, however, takes years of practice (figure 3-23).

iStockPhoto/Floriana

Figure 3-22 The darkest, most saturated spots are minimal and scattered about. All of the larger elements are pale, while aqua dominates and almost, but not completely, surrounds the green center. A twinkle of strong aqua punctuates the bottom, slightly off–center. All hang in beautiful balance, creating a fascinating visual adventure.

Francine Walker
Glacial Pools, 2010
30 x 20 x 0.8 cm
Sterling silver, aquamarine, amazonite, clear quartz, white agate, yellow turquoise, lime jade, freshwater pearl, blue topaz, peridot; soldered, rivited, hammered, wire wrapped, bezel setting
PHOTO BY ARTIST

Figure 3-23 In the art of ikebana, precisely arranged elements achieve exquisite assymetrical balance.

We can balance two items of unequal weight by moving the heavier inward toward the fulcrum (figure 3-24). Visually the same principle applies: Balance a large item by placing it closer to the center. Balance a smaller item by placing it closer to the perimeter. In the ikebana arrangement on the previous page, notice how the large flower is almost centered, while the smallest blossom defines the boundary line.

In her strung necklace, *Lily* (figure 3-25), Myra Schwartz positions large beads asymmetrically to bring attention to the center. The figure of the carved woman faces right, causing us to "read" the bead from left to right. The large bead on the right is positioned farther up the strand than the large bead on the left. This allows us more space to appreciate the intricacy of the focal bead's carving while forming an alluring balance.

Notice how Julia Dusman positions delicate curves and bold stones to fashion a sophisticated, mobile-like necklace in complex balance (figure 3-26).

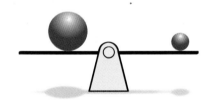

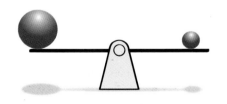

Figure 3-24

Because of your experience living the laws of physics, you can sense the balance in the drawing on the top, in which the unequally weighted items are a different distance from the fulcrum. Likewise you can sense the lack of balance in the drawing on the bottom. You know it's going to tip any minute now.

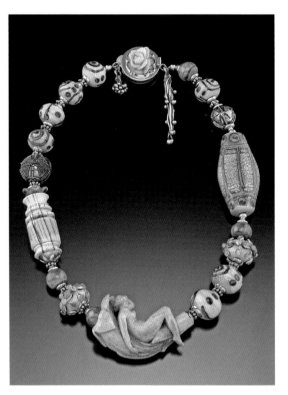

Figure 3-25

The two largest beads are balanced asymmetrically around the necklace. Because the center focal bead draws our attention to the right, the large bead on the right can be positioned higher than the one on the left, while maintaining equilibrium.

Myra Schwartz
Lily, 2007
50.8 x 3.8 x 3.8 cm
Antique meerschaum carving, lampworked glass beads, raku beads, antique ivory, vintage glass bead, sterling silver, carved bone, nylon- coated stainless steel wire; stringing
PHOTO BY LARRY SANDERS

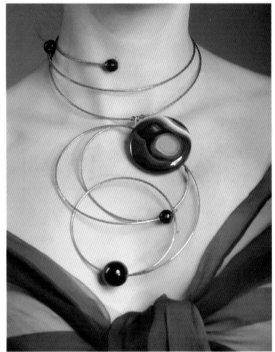

Figure 3-26

Like a meticulously balanced mobile, each cab is positioned to maintain equilibrium. The weight of the largest disk is counterpoised by all the swirling activity below and to the left.

Julia Dusman
Zodiac, 2010
32 x 10 x 2 cm
Agate, fluorite, crystal, glass, wire
PHOTO BY JENS LOOK

Figure 3-27

Balance through Texture and Pattern Texture and pattern create activity that engages our attention, thus appearing visually heavier than a plain area without texture. See this principle illustrated in beads in figure 3-18, page 50.

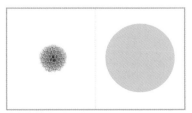

Figure 3-28

A larger expanse of texture is required to counterbalance the heavy visual weight of solid black.

Figure 3-29

On the left, all beads are the same size and relatively the same value. On the right, the textured beads are smaller than non–textured, while both are of similar value. Do you feel one is more balanced than the other? Which do you prefer and why?

Texture & Pattern

Texture and pattern are more interesting than a smooth surface. In Chapter 4 we'll discuss how they create movement and attract the eye. Such activity has the effect of weight, thus appearing visually heavier. Therefore, a small area bustling with texture or pattern will have more weight than a larger area with no texture or pattern (figure 3-27).

Juxtapose texture and pattern against smooth areas to create asymmetrical balance (figures 3-28 and 3-29).

The world of beads is one of texture and pattern. We need to be especially mindful of the visual weight they create. Lack of this awareness leads to overly busy and extremely heavy looking—if not physically heavy— jewelry. Often these pieces lack grace and balance.

Consider Heidi Kummli's necklace (figure 3-30). As with all of her work, the balance is thoughtfully arranged, and the result is a masterful composition. Even with an abundance of varying texture, pattern, and materials, there is no cacophony here. All is carefully ordered into peaceful and captivating balance.

Figure 3-30

The bib of the necklace features two smaller areas very busy with texture and pattern framing the larger, sparse design of the center. The repetitious fringe on the right counterpoints the fringe on the left, which is busy with layers of texture.

Heidi Kummli
Earth Spirit, 2011
30.5 x 20.3 x 1.3 cm
Seed beads, cabochons, vintage buttons, leather, mesh, ermine tails; bead embroidery
PHOTO BY ARTIST

Shape

A shape implies weight because it implies form. Even a simple, two–dimensional outline conveys visual weight. The same two–dimensional representation is visually heavier when the space within the lines is filled in with something other than white (figure 3-31).

Complex shapes with unexpected contours are more interesting than simple shapes, and will appear visually heavier (figure 3-32). As with texture and pattern, we can counterpoint busy shapes with active ones, and complex shapes with simple ones (figure 3-33).

Complex shapes as focal points are most prominently featured when surrounded and counterbalanced by simple shapes (figure 3-34).

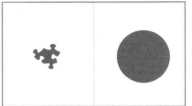

Figure 3-31

A line that circumscribes an area creates a shape, which imples visual weight. The shape is heavier when the area is filled with color (or a value other than white).

Figure 3-32

The weight of the complex shape on the left is visually equivalent to the larger simple shape on the right because it is more interesting, active, and engaging: it commands more attention.

Figure 3-33

The complex shape on the left half of the necklace is balanced on the right by three simple lines. The simple lines allow you to focus on that complexity, and provide pleasing asymmetrical balance.

Figure 3-34

Left: Repetition of complex shapes creates textural activity. The shapes become smaller as they move away from the center to allow prominence of the center shape.

Right: When you surround a complex shape with simple repeated shapes, you afford it prominence, making it a special attraction. The repeated shapes don't compete for attention.

Figure 3-35

The repetition of simple chain strands balances four asymmetrically arranged leaves.

Kristy Nijenkamp
Untitled, 2008
Focal element:
12 x 8 x 2.5 cm
Borosilicate lampworked beads, sterling; glasswork, wirework

Movement

The movement of visual activity, as we've seen with texture, pattern, and shape, demands attention. We'll delve into the concept of Movement in more depth in Chapter 4.

When it comes to weight, areas with more detail and intricacy appear heavier than areas that are less active. Intricate detail demands attention.

Kristy Nijenkamp's intricate lampworked leaves in figure 3-35 include movement in texture, shape, and positioning. Simple, straight chains are the perfect counterbalance to their activity. Heidi Kummli balances a concentration of activity and movement with a calmer neckstrap of repeating braids (figure 3-36).

Because there is no simple formula for achieving asymmetrical balance and we can't measure it, a degree of subjectivity is present. Where I may sense beautiful balance, you may not. Therefore, we need to use our own innate sense of balance to determine what feels balanced for each of us.

If you haven't explored asymmetry in your designs, try it! The tension and dynamism within asymmetry offer endless creative fascination. You'll find asymmetry a rewarding challenge that stretches your artistry.

Figure 3-36

The embellished left neckstrap is counterbalanced on the right by a more static assemblage of repeating braids. These gently nudge your attention down to the owl and provide a respite from the diagonal cascading activity of the entire necklace.

Heidi Kummli
Shapeshifter, 2010
45.7 x 8.9 x 5.1 cm
Seed beads, dagger beads, cabochons, bronze feather, fur; bead embroidery
PHOTO BY ARTIST

Visual Balance Study

IT'S A DILEMMA MANY OF US designers know well—precariously inching our way across the tightrope of pendant-to-neck-strap balance.

You'll know the artist didn't make it when a large pendant hangs heavily from a comparatively wimpy necklace strand. You can almost hear the necklace creaking as it strains under the weight of the pendant, digging a deep red groove in the back of the wearer's neck. And you fear that at any moment it'll break and beads will fly.

The opposite is just as disturbing: a dainty, simple pendant overpowered by thick, complex, densely beaded strands.

The focal bead is lost and you're now playing the confusing game known as "What Am I Supposed to Look At?"

SaraBeth Cullinan and I explored pendant-to-neck strap balance with her large bead-embroidered pendant.

SaraBeth Cullinan
Raspberry Sorbet, 2003
12.5 x 5.5 x 1.3 cm
Dichroic glass cabochon, seed beads, freshwater pearls, crystals; bead embroidery, peyote stitch, surface embellishment

1 Because of bead color, shape, and size variations in the neck strap, it competes with the pendant, which is already quite busy. The overall effect is visually confusing. The eye wants to follow the pale pink curve of the pendant down to the cab, but it can't because the necklace demands so much attention.

2 A neck strap of the dominant color creates a stronger piece. We now have the luxury of following the gentle S-shaped path downward to the cab. The width of the necklace (0.5 cm wide), however, is too thin to counterbalance the weight and substance of the pendant.

3 A thicker neck strap (1 cm wide), simple in color and design, creates the strongest piece. There is no competition between strand and pendant; we can focus on the beauty of the cab and the beadwork surrounding it.

Challenge Yourself

1 Symmetrical Balance

- Browse jewelry catalogues or websites for examples of vertical and horizontal symmetry. Find examples that simultaneously display both. Which kind of symmetry do you find more in earrings? Necklaces? Bracelets?

- Sketch several pair of earring designs using vertical symmetry.

- Do the same using horizontal symmetry.

- Sketch several pair of earring designs using both vertical and horizontal symmetry simultaneously.

- Vertical symmetry is common in necklaces and earrings. Horizontal symmetry isn't as common, and is rarely seen without vertical symmetry also being present. How do you feel about horizontal symmetry in a necklace or in earrings?

Do the images below display vertical symmetry, horizontal symmetry, both, or neither?

2 Asymmetrical Balance

Because you physically feel asymmetry, it helps to work with it when you're solidly "in your body," not in your intellectual, analytical mind, where many of us spend our days.

Drawing Asymmetrical Balance

Make 4 copies of the human form template for necklaces (page 84) and 12 copies reduced by 50%. Beginning with the half-sized templates, make rough, quick sketches of shapes and lines balanced asymmetrically representing necklaces. Use the shapes on page 83 for inspiration. Set a timer and spend no more than two minutes per drawing. After you've drawn 12, take a break of at least 30 minutes. Return and look at the pages. Do any of the compositions stand out as either exceptionally well or poorly balanced? Use your senses and intuition in addition to your analytical mind when assessing.

Select two of the drawings you feel are well balanced and re-draw them on the full-sized copy of page 84. Draw as slowly or quickly as you want. Can you improve the balance? Move, add, or subtract shapes. Notice how each change affects balance.

Choose two you feel are lopsided or awkward. Can you determine why they are unbalanced? Redraw them on the full-sized copy of page 84. Draw as slowly or quickly as you want. Can you improve the balance? Move, add, or subtract shapes. Notice how each change affects balance.

Think about how you would take one of these drawings from sketched idea to finished necklace. What kinds of beads, stitches, and techniques would you use? If the design presents the challenge of more weight being on one side than the other, how will you resolve it?

4 | Movement

Movement makes art come alive. We know physical movement well, the kind that occurs when beaded fringe sways or metal charms shimmy. Physical movement is obvious.

There is, however, another kind of movement—one less tangible, a movement that doesn't physically move. We *sense* this intangible movement more often than we see it.

Intangible movement occurs when a long, arcing line draws your eye from one end to the other. It engages you in its activity.

It is the movement—physical or intangible—in jewelry that initially calls to and captures the viewer: the sparkle of a reflective facet, the sinuous curve of an element, the beat-like percussion of a repetitive pattern.

Jewelry demands movement. If you can't incorporate physical movement into a piece, then the intangible form must be present. Without movement, a piece is static and, most likely, boring.

When you consciously develop intangible movement in your work, as Laurie Danch has (figure 4-1) you orchestrate the entire piece: how it is both seen and experienced. And you naturally unify the piece.

Figure 4-1

Above all else, the seductive allure of this collar is its undulating movement.

Laurie Danch
Red Ribbon Collar, 2010
20 x 20 x 1 cm
Dupioni silk, silk shibori ribbon, beading thread, crystals, pearls, rivolis, seed beads, sequins; bead embroidery, embellishment, peyote stitch
PHOTO BY MARTIN KONOPACKI

Figure 4-2

Each example beats a unique rhythm: the top is more staccato, the bottom is more fluid.

Top: Your focus travels from the edges inward, along diagonal rows that point toward the center and stop at each gold faceted bead. Ladder-like horizontal lines create secondary movement and rhythm.

Bottom: Rows repeating in the same diagonal direction create a more continuous movement. Your eye wants to "loop" from the end of each row to the beginning of the next.

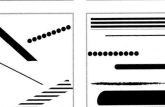

Figure 4-3

Direction of Line and Shape
Horizontal direction displays less movement than vertical. Diagonal direction displays the most movement.

Figure 4-4

Angles imply quick movement. The less organized and logical, the more erratic and chaotic the movement.

The principles discussed in previous chapters enhance movement. Let's explore ways to breathe life into your design through well-crafted, calculated movement.

DIRECTION OF LINE & SHAPE

Movement is implied by the direction of elements. The elements can be lines formed by rows or strands of beads, or shapes (figure 4-2).

Horizontal vs. vertical. Horizontal arrangements imply quiet repose, as if lying down to rest. Vertical arrangements imply action, like standing tall at attention (figure 4-3).

Diagonal. The most active arrangements are diagonal—they furnish tremendous movement. You've probably observed rain during a storm: the more active the storm, the more diagonal the rain. Notice the different movements in figure 4-3. Regardless of shape, width, or texture, can you sense how much more energetic the diagonal lines and shapes are? How much more serene the horizontal lines are?

Angles. The movement of angles, pointed and sharp, is rapid. They can convey steady or jarring rhythm, depending on how repetitive or sharp the angles are. When angles are not ordered into mathematically prescribed geometric shapes, movement becomes erratic (figure 4-4). When arranged in a geometrically logical fashion, shapes with angles can exhibit a steady, ordered, resolute movement, as they do in Kathy King's *Art Deco Bead Quilled Necklace* (figure 4-5).

Figure 4-5

Kathy King
Art Deco Bead Quilled Necklace, 2009
44 x 8 x .6 cm
Cylinder beads, glass beads, nylon thread; stacked quilling
PHOTO BY JASON DOWDLE

Curves. Coils, concentric circles, and curved lines and shapes provide tremendous movement—the tighter the curve, the faster the movement. The looser, the more serene (figure 4-6). Curved lines beckon you with movement slower than that of straight lines and edges. The curve is key to mystery.

Look at the vigorous directional movement of Suzanne Golden's *Black, White, and Red Bracelet* (figure 4-7). The most prominent force determining this movement is the curves, the diagonal rows ceaselessly circling around the piece.

REPETITION

Repetition emphasizes movement (figure 4-7). It's easy to sense the activity in Suzanne Golden's bracelet because of repeated elements, in this case the lines created by rows. Repetition creates a pattern which reinforces the movement of each individual line, shape, or element. Repetition also creates rhythm.

RHYTHM

In music, rhythm is marked by beats and the spaces in between them. Hip hop brandishes its rhythm in strong, bass-driven downbeats. A flowing, orchestral harp solo presents a rhythm built of swells and sweeps rather than percussive beats. They both offer a unique rhythm.

Visual rhythm is similar and is based on the repetition of elements and space seen rather than heard. The elements mark movement of the viewer's eye across a design, each one representing a beat, each interval between representing a pause. In visual art—jewelry included—you experience a more unified design when you can sense rhythm.

Visual rhythm is not only engaging, it's downright fun. Human beings were built to move. We love to dance. Visual rhythm indulges this drive. It pulls viewers in and keeps them there, "dancing" to the beat as they visually track the pulses.

Figure 4-6   I'm in love with curves, and they meander throughout my doodles, my paintings, and my beadwork. The lines on the cuff of my blue jeans embody intangible, curvilinear movement. See how they guide you up, down, and around, as if taking you on a sinuous walk?

Figure 4-7   Because of the placement of color in a pattern and its consistent repetition, your eye naturally follows the diagonal rows around and around the piece.

Suzanne Golden
Black, White and Red Bracelet, 2012
6 x 14.5 cm
Seed beads; tubular peyote stitch
PHOTO BY ROBERT DIAMANTE

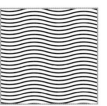

Figure 4-8

Which kind of repeated line makes you feel more calm? Which moves faster? Does one seem older than the other?

Figure 4-9

This flourish repeats similar elements, which produces a slightly unpredictable harmonious rhythm.

iStockPhoto/Miguel Malo

iStockPhoto/zentilia

Figure 4-10

Figure 4-11

The same visual, a fence, produces two different rhythms. What kind of rhythm do you sense in each? What changes in elements, direction, or space creates the rhythmic differences?

Figure 4-12 Elements that seem to be arranged randomly can create an enjoyably erratic rhythm.

Eleanor Lux
Always Collecting Anything, 2010
20 x 8 x 7.6 cm
Springs, O rings, washers; stringing, wirework
PHOTO BY CINDY MONCHILOV

Repetition of line, shape, or motif accentuates movement and creates rhythm and pattern. Notice the emotional effect of rhythm and how much emotion it can transmit (figure 4-8).

The repetition of similar elements that are not exactly alike produces a unique rhythm—one consistent and harmonious, yet not predictable (figure 4-9). In your jewelry designs, how can you repeat elements that are exactly alike, and elements that are similar, to achieve different rhythms?

SPACE AND SILENCE

Just as silence is an integral part of musical rhythm, space is an integral part of visual rhythm. Changing negative space alters rhythm. In the photos of the two fences (figures 4-10 and 4-11), notice the effect the amount of space between the posts has on rhythm. In the black fence, equal spacing of identical elements establishes a steady, moderately paced cadence. The white fence beats a quicker rhythm because the posts are much closer together. The rise and fall of the land creates an undulation of the entire line, suggesting a melodic, flowing rhythm.

Erratic rhythm is established by random positioning of elements and space, as in Eleanor Lux's bracelet (figure 4-12). She maintains unity by using similar shapes, sizes, colors, and elements with a hardware theme.

Intangible movement and visual rhythm dwell in the realm of feeling and the senses—slightly elusive, slightly mysterious, perfect for evoking mood. You can create tension by repeating angular elements. Smaller elements can create more rapid movement. Imbue a piece with tranquility by using long, curvilinear shapes and motifs in horizontal positions. To speed up movement, increase the repetition with progressively shorter intervals. To slow it down, do the opposite.

Complex rhythms are created by several repeating elements interacting with each other (figure 4-13, page 62).

Light plays a powerful role in jewelry. Our eye instinctively follows light just as it instinctively follows movement. Whether it flashes, shimmers, or dances off of jewelry, reflecting light is a form of rapid, eye-catching movement, and can be the most compelling movement of all.

As designers, we need to be aware of how much movement light contributes to a piece. The wearer moves, the jewelry moves, and light moves with both. We need to take all this movement into account as we design.

When every surface of every bead reflects light, as in jewelry made entirely of highly reflective, cut glass crystals, the result is perfect for the stage. Burlesque, drag shows, and the circus rely on rampant excess of reflective light to catch attention and dazzle.

In the jewelry we wear every day, however, such extravagant bling can visually distract to the point of overwhelming the viewer and eclipsing the wearer. The aesthetics of color, form, and design are lost in the radiant glare—all the eye can perceive is moving light. Sunglasses may be required!

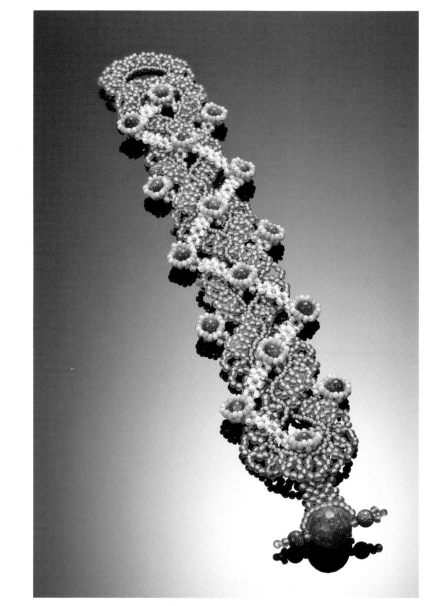

Figure 4-13   A complex rhythm of undulating curves and angular diagonals punctuated with stone accents.

Carol Wilcox Wells
Garden Lattice, 2010
18.4 x 3.8 cm
Cylinder beads, sunstones, jasper; chevron chain, right angle weave, peyote stitch
PHOTO BY SCOTT POTTER

I suggest this approach: Calculate the movement of light by how much the finish of the bead reflects or absorbs light. A faceted bead with a mirror finish is a busy bead indeed. A matte finished bead is more restful and calm. A sprinkling of sprightly faceted crystals among beads with a calm finish is a beautiful pairing because they complement each other, the matte forming a stationary background for the movement of light (figure 4-14).

Figure 4-14

Matte beads make the perfect foil to set off the sparkling movement of crystals and a dichroic centerpiece.

Frieda Bates
Chocolate Dream, 2011
42 x 6.7 cm
Dichroic glass, cylinder beads, faceted Czech glass; bead embroidery, peyote stitch

THE MOVEMENT OF PATTERN

To fill an empty space is a basic human impulse. We are compelled to embellish blank surfaces. Rice painters do it on a small scale; graffiti artists do it big.

There were no blank expanses of wall in my childhood home. The family joke was that if there was a blank space on the wall, it would soon be covered up with a painting. Almost every inch of my lifetime's worth of journals and notebooks are covered with doodles and drawings. Referring to what I wear or display in my house, a friend once remarked, "If it's stationary, Margie will cover it with beads or jewels."

When it comes to surface embellishment, bead artists may be more compulsive than most.

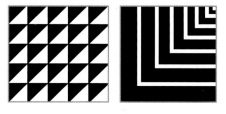

Figure 4-15

A simple pattern can be created by repeating one element in sequence. Create more movement by changing the dimensions of the repeated element.

Figure 4-16

Rhythm and movement created by pattern captivates our attention more than a flat smooth surface.

Figure 4-17

This complex pattern of repeating geometric shapes is stalwart and fixed, creating a steady, precise rhythm.

iStock photo/RosaFrei

Figure 4-18

Patterns formed organically intrigue us because they aren't entirely predictable. Notice how fluid the movement is compared to the geometric patterns.

Figure 4-19

Beads lined up to form a geometric pattern.

Margie Deeb
Stitched by SaraBeth Cullinan
Arabian Nights, 2009
17 x 4 cm
Cylinder beads; peyote stitch

Figure 4-20

Beads sewn in repeated scallop motifs and irregular curves make an organic pattern.

Jamie Cloud Eakin
Shell Game, 2011
17 x 4 cm
Everlasting shell, peridot jasper, freshwater pearls, seed beads; bead embroidery

Figure 4-21   Patterns within patterns and
undulating organic motifs
comprised of geometric units
make this bracelet a visual feast.

Met Innmon
Egyptian Waves Bracelet, 2008
19 x 4.4 x 0.7 cm
Seed beads, bugle beads, beading thread;
peyote, herringbone, and whip stitch
PHOTO BY LARRY HANSEN

Figure 4-22   Repeated components create an
overall pattern.

Met Innmon
Jolie Navette Necklace, 2012
20 x 16.5 x 0.6 cm
Seed beads, pearls; peyote stitch
PHOTO BY LARRY HANSEN

When we design a regular repeating sequence of elements, we've created a pattern. Patterns offer movement, visual excitement, intrigue, or beauty. They carry their own visual rhythm (figure 4-15).

Surface pattern is inherent in seed bead weaving, like it is in mosaic work or fiber weaving. The locking together of the beads and the minute spaces between them set up a predictable geometric pattern. If you weave only one color of seed beads in peyote stitch, you've created a surface pattern. As plain as you may find that swatch to be, it is more interesting than a swatch without the pattern the beadweaving creates. The pattern generated by peyote stitch has created surface texture that captures our attention (figure 4-16).

Patterns can be geometric, organic, or a combination of both. Geometric patterns (figures 4-15, 4-17, and 4-19) usually provide more orderly, predictable movement than organic patterns. Complex organic patterns hold interest longer because they're less predictable; the eye wants to follow and decipher the patterns (figures 4-18 and 4-20). Study the movement different patterns produce, taking notice of what kinds of lines and shapes make different rhythms.

Patterns can be constructed by repeating anything. Try repeating beaded elements, beaded lines, sizes, shapes, and colors. Variations are limited only by your imagination (figures 4-21 and 4-22).

THE MOVEMENT OF TEXTURE

Tactile texture is the sensual delight of working with beads. So delightful, in fact, that it is one of the reasons I began beading. Steeped in a life of drawing and painting, I craved an art form that appealed more to the sense of touch, one that gave the maker and owner an immediate sensual experience. We bead artists are in love with texture, and it gives us not only the gratification of visual movement, it also generates physical action. We love to touch jewelry, run our fingers across its surface, and savor the sensations caused by shape, size, and surface finish. At bead shows, everywhere you turn someone is reaching over and touching another person's bracelet or earrings.

Bead embroidery is the perfect medium for making jewelry that emphasizes texture as the focal point. There are few limits to what can be glued, sewn, and strung onto backing. As long as it fits within the scope of the project, it serves as a bead. In her body of award-winning work, Sherry Serafini has been known to include, among other items, erasers and miniature license plates to amp up drama and tactile intrigue. In figure 4-23, shells and fossils provide an abundant array of texture.

Figure 4-23   An abundant display of texture unifies the diverse components.

Sherry Serafini
Under the Boardwalk, 2008
35.6 x 12.7 x 0.6 cm
Cabochons, seed beads, pearls, shells, wooden discs; embroidered
PHOTO BY LARRY SANDERS

Figure 4-24

Visual texture is created by the rendering of hair: you can't actually feel it, but the inked lines represent it in such a way that you feel as if you can. You interpret it as a tactile sensation.

Margie Deeb
Untitled, 2009
15.2 x 23 cm
Ink on paper

Texture is a visual experience as well as a tactile one. When we see and interpret something as a tactile texture, but don't physically feel it, we refer to it as visual texture. Patterns create texture. You can "feel" or sense these textures without touching them (figures 4-24 and 4-25).

Don't settle for texture created only by your materials. Design visual texture into your work. Repeat motifs. Create patterns. Contrast design elements, all the while seeking to create intriguing visual, as well as tactile, texture with movement.

Figure 4-25

Run your fingers over the surface of this necklace, and you'll feel very little texture, as it is flat and smooth. But because of the intricate patterns woven into the image, visually this is a very textural piece.

Margie Deeb
Woven by Frieda Bates
Amira, 2007
48 x 13 x 0.2 cm
Cylinder beads, Czech glass; loom weaving

THE MOVEMENT OF COLOR

Color is frequency, it resonates. Even a single solid swath of color all by itself moves. Can you sense how yellow moves? Its movement is entirely different from that of blue (figure 4-26). If you sit quietly with patches of solid color you'll begin to sense their movement. As with all intangible movement, the movement of color is one that you experience, or sense, more than physically see with your eyes.

All color combinations involve movement. Pared down to its essence, color harmony is all about movement. When you become intimate with the language of movement, you open up a whole new way of working with color.

I approach my study of color movement as if I'm choreographing a dance. Within a scheme of limited and similar hues, such as monochromatic or analogous palettes (see pages 98 and 99), colors will move similarly, like rows of ballerinas fluidly tracing trajectories in unison (figure 4-27). The dynamic clash of complementary schemes can get as vigorous as Maori Haka dancing, with its deep chested chanting, hand slapping, and feet stamping.

Figure 4-26   Colors move. They are vibrations of light. Can you sense the different movement of each color? Which moves faster?

Figure 4-27

Analogous colors, like blues and greens, dance fluidly because they are similar. Complementary colors are so unlike each other that they pulsate and clash, making vigorous, exciting movement.

Carol Dean Sharpe
Untitled, 2012
19 x 5 x 0.1 cm
Cylinder beads; two-drop peyote stitch

The movement and color of dichroic glass seems to be born of another realm. The otherworldly, shimmering enchantment is a result of the interplay of micro-layers of metals and light that shifts depending on whether it is reflected or transmitted. The word "dichroic" means "two colors." Hold it one way and you see purple, tilt it and you see orange (figure 4-28). As certain wavelengths of light either pass through or are reflected, dichroic glass changes color. This creates pulsating movement.

Look at the movement of gradually changing colors (figures 4-29 and 4-30). Whether they shift lighter, darker, or to a different hue altogether, a movement more mesmerizing than that of precisely defined color regions emerges. Gradations of color generate movement because your eye follows the order of gradation, seeking the end. The gradation from lavender to deep purple pulls you into the depth of the bracelet in figure 4-32. Use gradation to guide the viewer's eye and create movement.

You can also create movement by strategically arranging areas of color, especially contrasting hues. In figure 4-33 your eye hops about the necklace, landing at the most vibrant spots—the highly contrasting pink beads.

Figure 4-28

Frieda Bates
Untitled, 2008
4.5 x 7 cm
Fused dichroic glass

Figure 4-29

As yellow shifts to blue your eye naturally follows the movement.

Figure 4-30

The gradual change in color draws you in as your eye is led from pink to white.

Figure 4-31

Several colors swirling into one another form a complex, moving dance that delights the eye.

Kristy Nijenkamp
Untitled, 2008
4 x 3 x 2 cm
Borosilicate glass

Figure 4-32

The incremental change in value, light to dark, draws your focus into the blue in the center of the ruffles.

Leslee Frumin
Calypso Cuff, 2008
19.1 x 4.1 cm
Seed and semi-precious beads, pearls, sterling silver; ndebele brick, ladder, and peyote stitches
PHOTO BY HAP SAKWA

Figure 4-33

A scattering of pink (green's complement) creates quick, light movement as your eye skims the piece. Lush texture increases the bustling activity.

Frieda Bates
Forever, 2011
96 x 2.5 x 2.5 cm
Cylinder beads, crystals, freshwater pearls; embellished spiral stitch

Figure 4-34

Marcia DeCoster
Tassel Necklace, 2012
Tassel: 8.9 cm long
Necklace: 76.2 cm long
Cylinder beads, crystals, glass pearls, silver, chain; cubic right angle weave, peyote stitch
PHOTO BY STEWART O'SHIELDS

PHYSICAL MOVEMENT

Swinging beaded fringe, tinkling metal charms, dangling sparkling crystals. For me, generating physical movement is one of the most sensual (and most fun) aspects of jewelry design. I love not only the feel and the look of moving jewelry, but the sound as well. Once, in a flea market in Santa Fe, I heard a melodious, rhythmical jangling just outside my view. I turned and saw a tall woman walking towards me, earrings swaying, a dozen necklaces bouncing, anklets swiveling around her boots, arms covered from elbow to wrist in bangles. I imagined her an exotic shaman from the far east, her jewelry imbued with magical powers. I no longer remember her face, but I'll never forget the music of her movement.

In *Marcia DeCoster's Beads in Motion,* she has engineered an array of beautiful jewelry with moving parts. The long, draping fringe of the Tassel Necklace (figure 4-34) provides elegant movement with a scintillating hint of glamour.

Physically moving jewelry requires calculated engineering and foresight. For practical reasons as well as aesthetic, we need to consider how a piece drapes and moves when on the body. I've owned jewelry that quickly became too painful to wear because the designer hadn't carefully thought out the consequences of its movement. Chapter 7: Jewelry & the Body explores these issues.

When you plan carefully, test-drive your creations, and make sure the wearing of your jewelry is pleasurable, moving parts add another dimension of sensual delight.

Movement, both physical and tangible, is the life force of jewelry. It acts like a charm, drawing people into its magical spell. To make your jewelry irresistible, infuse it with the magic of movement.

Movement Study

Leslee Frumin
Putting On the Ritz, 2012
38 x 20 x 0.5 cm
Pearls and briolettes, seed beads,
vermeil; right angle weave

LESLEE FRUMIN AND I EXPLORED movement through color and position with her necklace, *Putting On the Ritz*. I chose this piece because the design is simple and elegant, nothing pretentiously elaborate or fussy. This is a solid design that will endure. And the predictable pattern of the pearls creates the perfect canvas on which to paint movement.

Understand that little to no movement is not negative. Sometimes this may be exactly what you want: quiet understatement. In a monochromatic palette, *Putting On the Ritz* delivers this restrained sophistication (figure 4-36). In figure 4-37 Leslee emphasized the diagonal repetition, each peach row guiding your eye to the peach drop. Movement loops around the foundation of the pearls and circles fluidly around the neck. The subtle "stripes" make it a hint more casual.

In figure 4-38 we emphasized the inverted triangular repetition, with each copper-hued V pointing to a copper-hued drop. A third color entices your eye to hop about, seeking the pale accents. Livelier, less graceful movement creates a more playful piece.

Movement differs in each of these versions. How much and the kind of movement you want to create is your choice. You'll do your best when the choice is carefully planned.

Figure 4-36

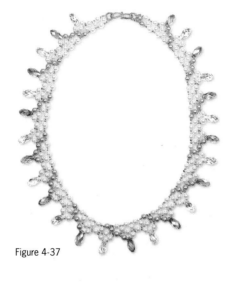

Figure 4-37

Figure 4-38

Challenge Yourself

1 Look for intangible, visual movement everywhere: jewelry, photos, the design of magazine spreads, the composition you see as you look out your window. What creates the movement...

- the direction of line or shape?

- pattern (geometric or organic or a combination)?

- texture?

- color (placement or actual hues)?

What kind of rhythm, if any, is present?

2 Step back and look at jewelry you have designed from a distance.

- What kind of movement does the overall piece present?

- What kind of rhythm, if any, do you sense?

3 Design a piece of jewelry that features movement.

- What kind of movement will you focus on first—direction? Pattern? Texture? Color?

- Will you use more than one kind of movement?

- Do you want the viewer to move steadily on a path to a fulfilling conclusion? Or amble in sinuous curves throughout the entire design?

- How can you employ pattern or texture to reach those ends?

- What kind of rhythm do you want viewers to feel when they see this?

5 | Shape

When looking at a piece of jewelry from a distance, its shape is the first thing you see. You can't discern individual beads or intricate surface embellishment. Your eye immediately perceives the essential shape (figure 5-1).

Jewelry makes a tactile, sensual experience out of shape. As we wear a carefully crafted shape of beauty—for that's what jewelry is—it becomes an expression and extension of who we are. Shape contributes to that expression.

 conveys a different message from ⬭

When you understand the visual language of shapes and what they convey emotionally, you'll be able to design jewelry that says exactly what you want it to. You'll be closer to creating the impact you want your designs to have.

I've seen bead artists challenged by the concept of shape design. Enthralled by the sparkle and color of beads, they enter a trance. Eyes glazed, fingers twitching, they want only to sew beads, many beads, many colors, many stitches, for as long as possible. I'm reminded of an experience I had with my young nephew. He desperately wanted me to teach him to draw a dragon. He was not, however, interested

Figure 5-1

When seen from a distance, all we recognize is the shape of a piece of jewelry. Only when we are closer can we distinguish elements such as texture, materials, design motifs, and surface embellishment.

Figure 5-2

Both the overall shape and the lampworked beads are elongated. Elongated shapes are flattering for jewelry because they draw attention vertically.

Maureen Buckley McRorie
Untitled, 2009
61 cm long
Silvered-glass lampworked beads, sterling and bali silver, crystals

in understanding the shape of the dragon—the placement of the wings in relation to the head, tail, and feet. He wanted to skip that "boring stuff" and draw hundreds of scales and fire billowing from the nostrils. I know that itch well! And it's natural for an 8-year-old to want to skip the underlying foundation to get to the "fun stuff." But that approach won't do for a jewelry designer.

Obsessed as we are with surface embellishment, it can be tempting for bead artists to minimize the importance of the shape of the jewelry we are designing so we can get to the "good stuff," the intricacies of stitch wizardry and surface ornamentation. When this kind of myopia is in place, design suffers. The most extraordinary beads woven into fascinating patterns amount to little if they are part of a sloppy or confusing shape.

So let's fall in love with shapes. Let's learn all we can about their movement, style, and language. Our jewelry will be more beautiful because of it.

Very Vertical

Fashion convention is to elongate and use any contrivance necessary to draw attention vertically. We are vertical creatures, much taller than wide. So vertical compositions are a more natural format for necklaces and earrings than those with horizontal emphasis (figure 5-2).

When the body is wider, wider necklaces can be worn, as long as the width is balanced with ample depth. Don't emphasize width unless you want the eye to be drawn across the body, accentuating girth.

In this simple example the vertical shapes—those longer than they are wide—feel more natural and are more flattering to our vertical human form.

Shape and line are part of a visual language that conveys psychological states and lends emotional nuances to a composition. Shapes are composed of lines, curves, or angles. Let's understand these first, then examine specific shapes.

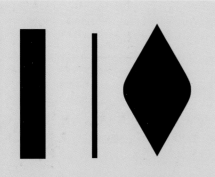

Vertical lines and shapes convey stability and strength, like sentinels standing tall and keeping vigil.

Horizontal lines and elements are very stable while conveying tranquility and peace. They imply quiet repose, like a landscape.

Diagonal lines and shapes are the most active, transmitting tremendous movement. In a storm, the more active the wind, the more diagonal the rain.

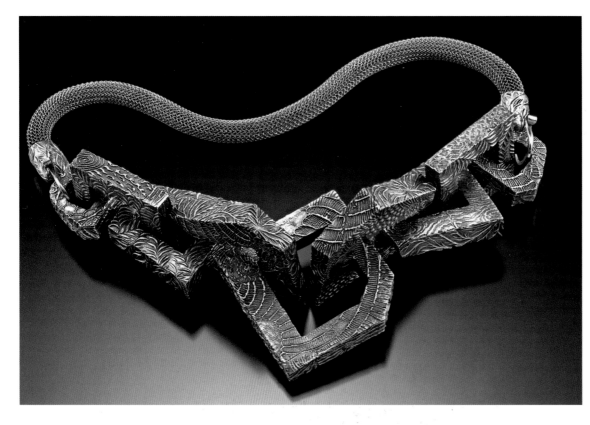

Juxtapose masculine and feminine shapes to achieve dynamic tension
Straight edges, sharp angles, and thick solids create a muscular style. A soft and supple curving neckstrap, along with an organically patterned surface texture, tempers the masculinity.

Barbara Becker Simon
Big Links, 2006
50.8 cm long
Biggest link: 5.7 x 5.7 x 0.9 cm
Fine silver, stainless steel, sterling silver
PHOTO BY LARRY SANDERS

Angular lines, shapes, and sharp points are more masculine than curves. They are lively and youthful, yet sometimes convey erratic or angry energy as well.

Curves are feminine and full of movement. They suggest warmth, comfort, and mystery. Since our eyes enjoy following curves, using them inherently imbues movement.

Organic lines and shapes can be flowing, curving, and uneven. Because they often represent shapes in nature, their familiarity can be comforting. They are natural and convey growth, life, and spontaneity.

Use shapes and lines that convey the same messages to achieve harmony
In this symbolic representation of the Goddess, organic, flowing curves, rounded shapes, and a spiral suffuse this necklace with feminine warmth and sensually.

Margie Deeb
Woven by Frieda Bates
Matriarch, 2007
53.5 x 10.8 x 0.6 cm
Glass beads

Don't mistake simplicity of shape for bad or lazy design. Simplicity of shape is easier for the eye to assess, and is often the most beautiful form. If a shape is too complex, it risks becoming confusing and unrecognizable. Let's look at basic geometric shapes and what they convey.

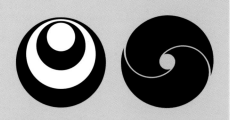

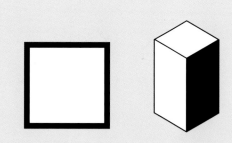

Circle

wholeness or completion, femininity, softness, protection, warmth, comfort, celestial, eternity, continuity; circles draw the viewer into their center, and convey movement.

Square & Rectangle

stability, order, organization, efficiency, rigid, solid, static

Triangle

stability, balance, strength, dynamic tension, mystery

Circles Circles connected by circles keep your eye looping around the entire bracelet

Jeannette Cook
Blings & Rings Bracelet, 2009
17.8 x 0.3 cm
Seed beads, crystals, anodized aluminum jump rings; right angle weave and netting
PHOTO BY ARTIST

Squares Separated by rectangles, the squares in this choker create a steady, marching rhythm around the neck.

Candie Cooper
Rococo Ribbon, 2012
Bead size: 1.7 x 1.7 x 8 mm
Slider beads, ribbon, vintage buttons, silver findings; stringing
PHOTO BY STEWART O'SHIELDS

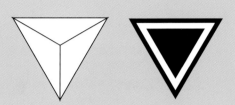

Inverted Triangle
intrigue, precarious balance, dynamic tension, mystery

Spiral
transformation, movement, growth, energy, creativity, trust during change

Cross
spirituality, healing, self, nature, wisdom, transition, balance, faith, unity, temperance, hope, a higher power or being

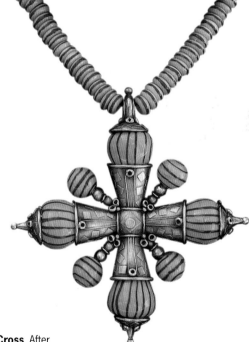

Triangles Progressively smaller as they descend, the inverted triangles in this pendant offer intriguing visual repetition.

Diane Fitzgerald
Triangle Bezel, 2009
Cylinder beads, vintage buttons; peyote stitch, stringing
PHOTO BY LYNNE HARTY

Greek Cross After circles, crosses are one of the first symbols drawn by children of all cultures. A Greek cross is formed when all arms are of equal length.

Barbara Becker Simon
Maltese Cross, 2012
Cross: 10.2 x 10.2 cm
Lampworked glass beads, fine silver
PHOTO BY BABETTE BELMONDO

THE BEAUTY OF GEOMETRIC SHAPES

Because of their corners and straight edges, geometric shapes provide an ordered stability. All but one of the shapes in figure 5-3 are instantly familiar, leaving us to ponder the unusual shape above the triangle.

In figure 5-4 the geometric brick-like grid provides order and stability to the unfamilair geometric shapes. Because the shapes lack the curves that traditionally define flowers, we're forced to look carefully to discover the floral motif.

The necklace in figure 5-5 offers comfort in the predictable shape of rectangles.

Figure 5-3

Diane Fitzgerald
Tuareg Pendant, 2009
Cylinder beads, copper beads, end caps, rondelles; tubular herringbone, peyote, brick stitch
PHOTO BY LYNNE HARTY

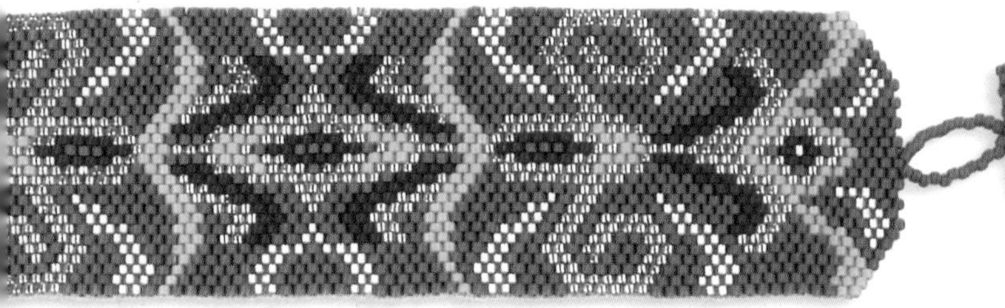

Figure 5-4   The brick-like configuration of the peyote stitch lends itself to beautiful geometric patterns.

SaraBeth Cullinan
Untitled, 2010
17 x 4 cm
Cylinder beads; peyote stitch

Figure 5-5

Kristy Nijenkamp
Untitled, 2011
48 cm long
Dyed howlite, crystals, sterling; stringing

THE BEAUTY OF ORGANIC SHAPES

Organic shapes offer natural movement. When organic shapes are abstract (figure 5-6) they are less predictable than representational shapes. When aesthetically pleasing, they can fascinate and beguile, for they hint at mystery.

When they are representational, like shapes of leaves and flowers (figures 5-7 and 5-8), a sense of growth and life accompany them. They provide the comfort of the natural world: We know the shape and can relate to it.

Figure 5-6

Margie Deeb
Woven by Frieda Bates
Twisted Neon, 2008
Pendant: 28 x 11.5 x 0.4 cm
Cylinder and pressed glass
beads; loom weaving

Figure 5-7

Stephanie Sersich
Party Necklace, 2010
19 x 20.5 x 2.5 cm
Handmade glass beads and button, Lucite, glass and
stone beads, floss and waxed linen; knotted
PHOTO BY TOM EICHLER

Figure 5-8

Sara Oehler
Untitled, 2008
Bracelet: 19 cm long
Earrings: 3.2 cm long
Tourmaline, olivine, crystals, sterling,
beading wire
PHOTO BY BRIAN CLARK

The first thing your eye comprehends is overall shape. Let's examine this concept. These necklaces are based on simple shapes, alone or in combination. The silhouette below each photo isolates this overall shape, bringing it into focus.

The Shape of a Line

The silhouette of a strand of beads looks less like a shape and more like a line circling the neck. Very thick strands of large beads and multistrands (as in the necklace to the right) have more volume. Their silhouette is more of a shape than a line.

Jamie Hogsett
Untitled, 2010
31 cm long
Polymer clay, coral, turquoise, original clasp, beading wire; stringing

Space is Part of the Shape

A multistrand necklace composed of several or many strands appears as a single shape, even when there is space between the strands. When designing multistrands, aim first for flattering shape, then beautiful proportions and proper drape.

SaraBeth Cullinan
Lavender Morning, 2009
48 cm long
Freshwater pearls, gold-filled and vermeil beads, glass crystals and pearls, faceted amethyst, lampworked beads; stringing

All Components Create Shape

A crescent around the neck is simple, feminine, and regal. The spaces within the design are components of its shape. The bottom of the spikes create a curving line that contains the overall shape. This design is flattering to necks that are medium to thin in width and length.

Margie Deeb
Mermaid's Collar, 2008
29 x 29 x 0.7 cm
Glass beads, sterling; wirework

Shape Can Flatter Certain Necklines

An elegant, elongated crescent flatters thick necks because it draws attention vertically, lengthening the neck.

Margie Deeb
Sparkling Draped Loop Collar, 2008
32 x 27 x 0.7 cm
Glass beads; right angle weave, stringing

The Eye Fills in the Gaps

Gaps between the cylindrical coral pieces remain part of the larger shape, which the eye perceive as a wide, flattened disk with the center hollowed out.

Kristy Nijenkamp
Untitled, 2010
Focal bead: 9 cm x 3.5 cm
38 x 29 x 1.5 cm
Red coral, borosilicate glass, black agate; stringing, lampwork

Simple to Complex

The outline of this silhouette is constructed of three simple shapes: a crescent, circle, and inverted triangle. The resulting compound shape is beautiful in its symmetry and movement. The bottom point elongates. The curve of the upper cab creates a sensual counterpoint to the dip between the clavicles.

Frieda Bates
Yellow and Chiffon, 2010
39 x 20 x 1 cm
Handmade dichroic cabochon, crystals, seed beads; bead embroidery, fused glass

We long for shapely form. Be it visual, be it in language, story, or in music, we long for shape...beautiful shape. But what makes a beautiful shape?

...the balance of flowing curves and straight edges?

...the surprise of a curve changing directions?

...the journey your eyes take as they trace the boundaries?

...the peacefulness of its symmetry?

...the dynamism of its asymmetry?

Look more closely at shapes you like and consider why they captivate you.

Consider the simple and complex shape templates in figure 5-9. Notice that many feature graceful, feminine curves. Some taper to a point either at the top or bottom, conveying elegance. Converging points provide movement, continue the visual path, and echo the vertical form of the human body.

Use these templates for earrings, pendants, components, or beads made of polymer clay or wire. Don't forget to try them upside down. Repeat them in different sizes, positions, and arrangements to make patterns or larger shapes. If you work primarily in seed beads, try building these shapes in different stitches and techniques.

Repeat Shapes By gradating and alternating colors of the same shape and separating them with small discs, Sarah Shriver creates a simple, yet extraordinarily elegant composition.

Sarah Shriver
Petal Bracelet, 2008
Beads 3.8 x 2 cm
Polymer clay, elastic cord, brass spacer beads
PHOTO BY GEORGE POST

Figure 5-9   How can you combine or repeat these shapes
for more complex beauty?
What can you create with them that is innovative
and intriguing?

SHAPE & THE HUMAN FORM

If you haven't designed jewelry based on shape, you'll be surprised at how this approach can help you become a better designer. You become focused on the big picture first, then smaller elements and technique later. Start by thinking about overall shape. What shapes do you like? If a circle has special meaning for you and you want to challenge yourself, consider adding other shapes to the circle to make a more interesting silhouette.

Sketch shapes and designs on the human form, especially when designing necklaces (figure 5-10). While in this sketching phase, move decisions about surface embellishment and color aside. Now is not the time for that. Focus on the big picture: overall shape. Use the line drawings on this page as jewelry sketching templates. Rather than black line drawings, these are light gray so they don't overpower your sketches.

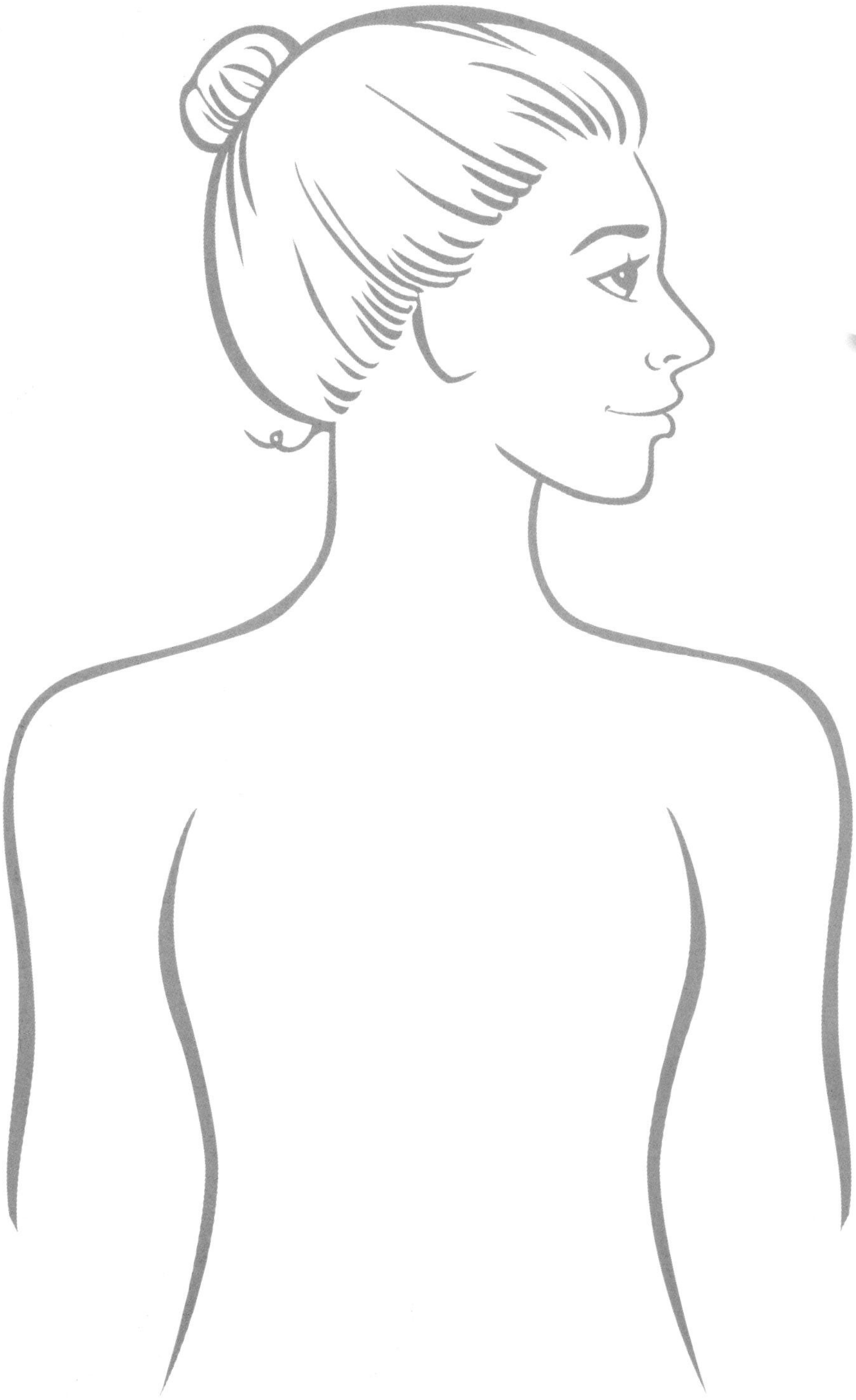

Figure 5-10

During your design stage, sketch directly on images of the human form so you'll have a more complete sense of how your shapes interact with the body.

Use the four line drawings on these pages as templates for sketching necklaces, earrings, bracelets, and rings on a human form.

See page 57 for an exercise in using this form.

You have my permission to photocopy, enlarge, and reduce these images as often as you like.

Invite shape into your repertoire of design tools. If you're itching to try a new stitch, challenge yourself to engineer it into several shapes. If you're hankering to make a necklace around a particular focal bead, surround it with beautiful shapes that will enhance its form. Try laying the focal bead on paper and drawing shapes around it to learn what works.

Seek the beauty of shape—look for it everywhere. Let shape guide your creativity and inspire new design. Now that you speak its visual language, you can say exactly what you want to through shape.

Shape Study

Candace Cloud McClean
Abundant Life, 2012
37 x 18 x 0.8 cm
Handmade glass beads,
crystals, sterling; wirework,
stringing

Version 1

CANDACE CLOUD MCLEAN AND I EXPLORED shape through four versions of her colorful cane glass necklace, *Abundant Life.* The unusual shape of the necklace is intriguing; its asymmetry invites our rapt attention. The piece is beautifully unified through color, materials, and texture.

One area, however, distracts from the overall harmony: the house-like shape inadvertently formed at the intersection of the three branches. Outlined by beads, this shape is one of negative space. Because it's an unusual shape, positioned off-center, and larger than the other negative spaces in the necklace, this shape stands out. We explored this issue, born of construction necessities, in this study.

Version 2

In the second version we elongated the overall shape by replacing the triangular bead at the bottom with a lush tassle of beads.

We repeated the bunched-bead foundation on both sides in order to eliminate the house-like shape. Now that the two sides are identical, we no longer have an asymmetrical piece. The overall shape is symmetrical. We traded the unusual intrigue of asymmetry for visual balance. Though this solves the issue of the distracting shape in the upper center of version 1, we've made a very different necklace.

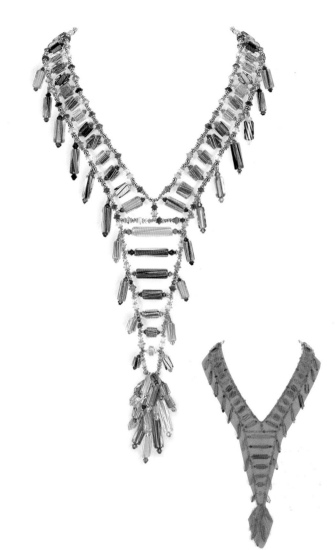

Version 3

In this third version we used the ladder motif on the entire necklace. This eliminated movement and created a more static design. It also created another house-like shape at the intersection of the three branches. I find this less distracting than the one in the first version because it is symmetrical and not quite as large.

Version three is more conservative than the first two versions. It's not quite as playful, and perhaps more elegant.

We've kept the tassle of beads at the bottom to elongate the shape.

Version 4

We feel the design of version 3 doesn't reflect the lively nature of the cane beads. It is too static. To reintroduce movement, we hung cane beads, like vertical drops of fringe, at regular intervals. We brought back the movement and playfulness absent in version 3. These drops serve another function—they draw attention away from the house-like shape at the intersection.

In these four iterations we solved issues and explored others. What we didn't achieve was a construction method that resolves the house-like shape while maintaining the initial asymmetrical design. When venturing into innovative design, more often than not we're met with construction challenges that affect the unity. How would you respond to this challenge?

Challenge Yourself

To expand your idea of what shapes can be and how they can be made, you're going to make as many new shapes from one shape as you can. Then, try working with two.

First, select one shape from page 83. Use the following methods to construct new shapes, designs, or motifs:

repeat   overlap

rotate   reflect

reverse   scale

subtract   combine

Don't forget, you can make asymmetrical shapes, too!

How might you use the new shapes as designs or motifs in jewelry?

How can you construct the shapes with beads, polymer clay, metal, or wire?

All of the examples on this page are built from the shape at the top of the page.

Technical Tips

Here are several ways to go about this challenge:

- Use a copier or scanner to duplicate the shape and print it out at different sizes. Cut the shapes out and glue or tape them in position on another sheet of paper.

- Use tracing paper to draw the shapes you've printed.

- Import the scanned image into a graphics or layout program and play to your heart's content.

Now that you've explored one shape, think about working with two. I've taken two of my favorite shapes, a circle and a teardop, and combined them into shapes I find beautiful, especially for jewelry. (OK, I cheated a bit: I pinched the teardrop into a paisley shape on the far right in the center row). These shapes can stand alone, or be repeated in necklaces or bracelets. What can you create using two of your favorite shapes?

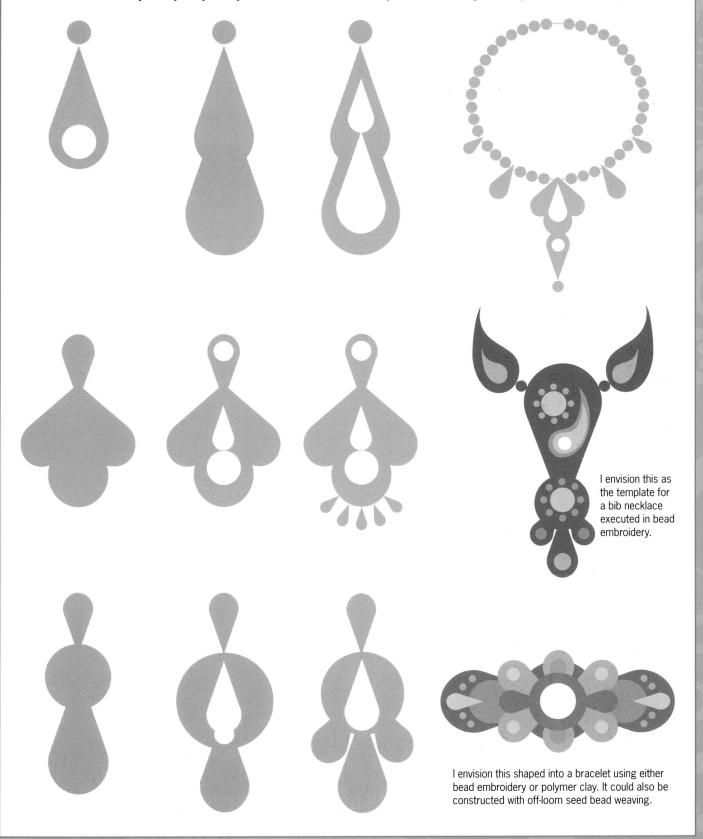

I envision this as the template for a bib necklace executed in bead embroidery.

I envision this shaped into a bracelet using either bead embroidery or polymer clay. It could also be constructed with off-loom seed bead weaving.

6 | Color

I live and breathe the study of color. So am I biased when I say color is the strongest determinant of a first impression? No. That's a proven fact. When looking at a piece of beadwork, a viewer will accept or reject it in less than 30 seconds. The colors you use account for 60 percent of that decision.

How many times have you seen a beautiful necklace ruined by lifeless color? Or a simple piece raised to the extraordinary by unusual use of color?

Our reaction to color is emotional and visceral. Our "heart" reacts strongly and we feel the response in our bodies.

Likewise, the colors we choose for our jewelry elicits emotional, gut-level responses from others. Color, and color alone, can infuse your creations with the ability to astonish.

Color is critical to you, the artist, because it is one of the most powerful notes in your artistic voice. Your unique sense of color, cultivated and nurtured, becomes a signature of who you are.

Triad and True A complementary triad of three slightly lightened hues accented with black and gold make a distinctive color scheme.

Candace Cloud McLean
Necklace for Mary, 2012
40 x 2 x 2 cm
Pressed and foiled glass, resin, crystals, vermeil; stringing

Simplicity can be the most elegant color solution Two colors, soft coral and gold, combine for elegance and sophistication.

Margie Deeb
Mandala Earrings, 2011
8 x 3.7 cm
Vintage buttons, epoxy and brass drops, glass seed beads; embroidery and stringing

Busy composition and simple color Because the structure of this bracelet, with its open spaces, angled lines, and different sized spheres, is full of physical and intangible movement, a simple color scheme works best.

Valérie MacCarthy
Sunset, 2007
19.4 cm
Shell pearls, smoky quartz, gold-filled chain and wire; wire wrapping
PHOTO BY STEWART O'SHIELDS

A MIGHTY LANGUAGE

Color is a language. You've heard that before, but think about what this means: Color "speaks" to you (people feel very strongly about color, just ask), it conveys mood, it gives you impressions, it makes you feel a certain way, it influences your thoughts and decisions. It does what language does in the most subtle and the most strident ways.

How long would it take you to master the speaking, hearing, and writing of a foreign language? You can spend your whole life learning and mastering this language. Still, there will be more to learn about the powerful impact of color. Entire books have been written specifically about color and beadwork.

Because we're limited, for this experience, to only one chapter, we'll focus on a broad overview of how to use color to create the impact you want to have in your jewelry.

Becoming Color Conscious

First and foremost it's important to be conscious of what draws you to a color or a color combination. Don't stop at "it's a pretty combination" to explain the attraction. What makes it pretty? How do you feel when you look at it? What about it makes you feel that way? What does it inspire in you?

Being aware of the "why" will help when you're deciding what you want to convey with your jewelry and your color choices.

When you're more conscious, alive, and awake to color, you fill your work with more of your voice—it has much more vitality. And the voice and vitality of a piece of art or jewelry is truly what speaks to us.

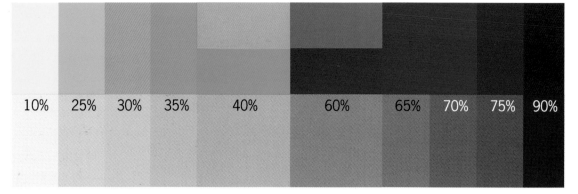

| 10% | 25% | 30% | 35% | 40% | 60% | 65% | 70% | 75% | 90% |

Figure 6-1   Here are the members of the modern ink-based wheel in value progression, from light to dark, left to right. Just beneath them, swatches of their corresponding grayscale values are shown. Orange and green are the same value (40% of solid black), as are the blue and magenta (60% of solid black).

Does any of this progression surprise you? Yellow has the highest value of all the pure hues; it is the lightest color. Purples and blues, depending on their shade, have the lowest value.

PROPERTIES OF COLOR: VALUE

The most important property of color is its value: how dark or light a color is. Yellow has the highest value of all the pure hues; it is the lightest color. Purples and blues, depending on their shade, have the lowest value; they are the darkest colors. You can discern value more easily when hue is removed. In figure 6-1, look at the top row of colors and their corresponding values beneath. Yellow is equal to 10% black, a very light gray; violet corresponds to 90% black. Notice the vast difference in value.

Value Is Relative

Value changes under different intensities of illumination. A black charcoal briquette in the brilliant sunlight appears to be a very light gray (figure 6-2). Likewise, the whitest cotton sheet seems dull gray in a dimly lit room (figure 6-3). In the top photo, I've sampled how black appears to the eye; I've done the same in the bottom photo with white. When pulled out of context, you can see they are not at all what they appear. See how your mind sees what it wants to see?

Value is also relative to the color against which it is placed. For example, next to dark blue beads, yellow will appear lighter than it does when set against pale orange beads.

How to apply this concept? Be aware that lights will appear lighter against darks, and vice versa. When designing areas you want to draw attention to first, use this to your advantage, as Christine Marie Noguere does (figure 6-4). To play down areas, use colors similar in value, those with less contrast.

Black

Figure 6-2

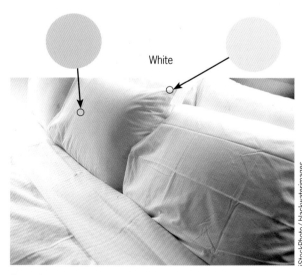

White

Figure 6-3

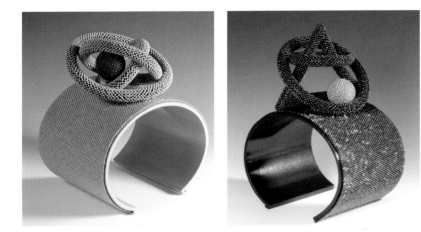

Figure 6-4   **Christine Marie Noguere**
LEFT: *Titania (Jewelry for Giants, No. 5)*, 2007
RIGHT: *Arc to Arcturus (Jewelry for Giants, No. 6)*, 2011
23 x 19 x 15 cm
Cylinder and seed beads, cork ball, butyl cord, maple wood, pearlescent paints;
right-angle weave, peyote stitch, bent, laminated, painted
PHOTOS BY PHIL POPE

Value Contrast

The contrast of light and dark colors is one of the most powerful visual contrasts you can create. Strong value contrast creates strong impact (figure 6-5). Minimal value contrast creates a more subtle visual impact (figure 6-6).

As we discussed in Chapter 2, Focal Point and Emphasis, you want to guide your viewer's eye with strategically arranged value contrast. The eye is often attracted first to the lightest area within a piece, so place the lightest and brightest beads where you want the viewer to look first. On the other hand, if a piece is all light beads with one dark bead, the eye will go straight to the dark bead, because that's where the most contrast lies.

Christine Marie Noguere uses value contrast to rivet your focus in each of her sculptural bracelets (figure 6-4). On the left she draws your eye to the darkest color, red, because it contrasts starkly against the light blue. In the bracelet on the right she's made you focus on the brightest area by surrounding it with dark. In both she employs the technique of value contrast for attention.

Figure 6-5

Sandy Lent
Anemone Pods, 2011
40.7 x 6.4 x 6.4 cm
Lampworked and acid-etched beads
PHOTO BY RYDER GLEDHILL

The Harmony of Similar Value

Colors similar in value are naturally harmonious. The light values in figure 6-6 are very similar, so they're naturally harmonious. Fortunately, there is also enough value contrast to keep the piece lively. Using a palette of colors too close in value can be boring when there's not enough contrast to attract attention.

Train yourself to discern and understand the value of colors by examining photographs. Note the distribution of light and dark. Squinting helps visually separate lights from the darks. Determine the lightest value, then the darkest, and finally look for tonal differences in between.

Figure 6-6

Patricia Zabreski Venaleck
Spring Leaves, 2009
50.8 x 2.5 x 1.3 cm
Lampworked beads, crystals
PHOTO BY JERRY ANTHONY

Properties of Color: Hue

When you ask "What color is that bead?" you want to know the *hue*. If I tell you it's teal, I'm not really telling you what color it is, I'm referring to the *hue*. The terms "hue" and "color" are often used interchangably. Even though they they don't mean exactly the same thing, using "color" when you mean "hue" is generally acceptable. For this chapter, however, as we discuss color's intricacies, we need to distinguish between properties such as hue and color so we can be more precise.

As I say in my classes, hue is the color of a color. It describes in a word the general range of color: red, blue, green, etc. That's how simple this color property is.

Properties of Color: Intensity

When you say a color is a "dull blue," the word "dull" refers to the *intensity* of the blue hue. Also referred to as chroma or saturation, *intensity* describes the degree to which a color is pure or not pure. Intense colors are fully saturated with their pure hue (figure 6-7). Less intense colors are less saturated, less pure (figure 6-8). The lowest intensity colors of all are neutral colors, like grays, beiges, and certain browns.

Don't confuse intensity with value. Remember, value is the relative lightness or darkness of a color.

Value can influence the intensity of a color, but a darker hue (lower value) does not necessarily mean lower intensity (muted or dull). Pure violet is dark; it has a low value. And it is an intense, fully saturated color. Intense colors can have a high or low value: they can be light or dark.

When you compose a palette that contrasts low and high intensity

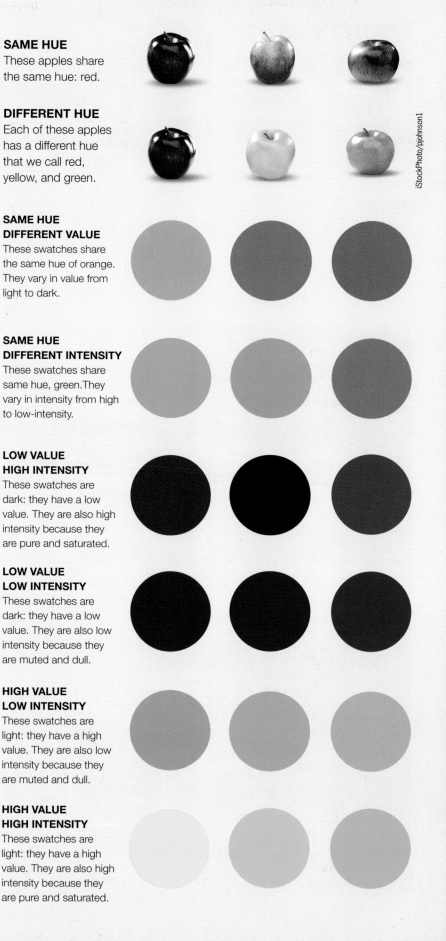

Properties of Color
Understand how the various properties of color work together

SAME HUE
These apples share the same hue: red.

DIFFERENT HUE
Each of these apples has a different hue that we call red, yellow, and green.

iStockPhoto/pjohnson1

SAME HUE DIFFERENT VALUE
These swatches share the same hue of orange. They vary in value from light to dark.

SAME HUE DIFFERENT INTENSITY
These swatches share same hue, green. They vary in intensity from high to low-intensity.

LOW VALUE HIGH INTENSITY
These swatches are dark: they have a low value. They are also high intensity because they are pure and saturated.

LOW VALUE LOW INTENSITY
These swatches are dark: they have a low value. They are also low intensity because they are muted and dull.

HIGH VALUE LOW INTENSITY
These swatches are light: they have a high value. They are also low intensity because they are muted and dull.

HIGH VALUE HIGH INTENSITY
These swatches are light: they have a high value. They are also high intensity because they are pure and saturated.

Figure 6-7 **Carole Horn**
Manhattan Flower Garden Necklace, 2010
24.1 x 24.1 cm
Seed beads; herringbone, peyote and various stitches
PHOTO BY D. JAMES DEE

colors, you can create sophisticated and dramatic results. High intensity colors come alive juxtaposed against low intensity colors. Practice stringing high and low intensity colors side by side and watch the colors shift. The high intensity hues of the bracelet in figure 6-9 appear sparkling bright against an array of lower intensity, neutral tones.

Study the effects of vivid colors woven into low-intensity palettes. Bright colors stand out against low intensity backgrounds, particularly when the colors are complements of each other.

A Note about Thread Color

You already know that reflected light and background color markedly affect—sometimes even drastically change—the perceived color of glass beads, especially transparent beads. Likewise, thread color impacts the bead's perceived color. A bead's intensity can be strongly affected by thread color. Dark thread lowers the intensity (slightly dulls the color) of transparent and semi-transparent beads—especially seed beads, because they are so small in relation to the thread. White thread used in the same beads increases their intensity, because more light and color is reflected back to the eye.

Figure 6-8 **Jamie Hogsett**
Coastal Day, 2011
49.5 cm long
Polymer clay, porcelain, kazuri beads, stones, wood, glass, metal

Figure 6-9 **Patricia Ventura Parra**
Cocoon Necklace, 2011
44 cm long
Handmade Egyptian paste beads, handmade/thrown Faenza clay elements, handmade wool beads, carded wool, industrial felt string; fired, knotted, sewn
PHOTO BY ARTIST

Properties of Color: Temperature

Working with temperature is one of my favorite aproaches to color because it involves more of your senses. A color's temperature can be sensed as well as measured. Warm colors stimulate circulation. Cool colors slow it down.

On the color wheel, when a hue is closer to orange (or red, depending on the wheel), it is warmer. When closer to blue (or cyan, depending on the wheel), it is cooler. Like fire and ice, red-orange and blue-green are the hottest and coolest colors on the wheel, respectively.

It's important to understand that all hues have warm and cool variations. Some blues are warmer than other blues. Some reds are cooler than other reds.

Warm colors are dynamic. Reds, yellows, and oranges cover the packages in the grocery store aisles so that they'll stand out. Use warm and hot colors to get attention.

Cool colors are calming and refreshing. You'll see them used in packaging of products that convey a sense of refreshment, cleanliness, and soothing—like pain-relieving gels. Use cool colors to convey peace, harmony, and purity.

Surface finish affects a bead's perceived color temperature. Highly reflective surfaces appear hotter because they are active and reflect light. Luster or pearlescent finishes appear slightly cooler because they absorb light.

The animated movie *The Polar Express* artfully works warm against cool colors with enchanting results. Its expansive vistas of snowy blues would leave viewers shivering if not for the luminous amber and yellow scenes of the train's interior. Because of the back-and-forth and side-by-side juxtapositions of hot and cold colors, the whole movie visually sparkles.

Kristy Nijenkamp sandwiches color blocks of cool blue between hot yellow and orange for an arresting palette (figure 6-10).

Create depth and vitality by mingling different temperatures of one color family. For example, interlace warm yellow-greens with cool blue-greens and teals.

iStockPhoto/Mik122

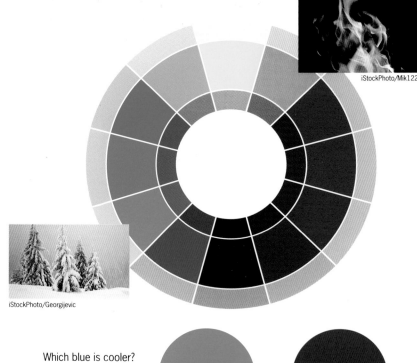

iStockPhoto/Georgijevic

Which blue is cooler? Hint: The one on the right contains magenta, bringing it closer to orange.

Which red is cooler? Hint: The one on the left contains more yellow, bringing it closer to orange.

CREATING COLOR PALETTES

Now that you understand the main properties of color—value, hue, intensity, and temperature—let's explore how to use them with the color wheel to make our jewelry extraordinary. After this, you need never suffer from *hyperchromacombinia* (fear of combining colors) again!

As you set out to design your own color palette, ask yourself the following questions:

• *How do I want the person wearing this piece of jewelry to feel?* Happy? Playful? Delighted? More alive? Glamorous? Proud? Gorgeous? Confident? Exquisite? Romantic? Sexy? Luxurious?

• *What do I want this jewelry to convey?* A sense of beauty or wonder? A sense of mystery or magic? A feeling of wholeness? A sense of empowerment? Peace?

Proceed only after you've integrated the answers into your heart and mind. Feel it in your body as you design and create. Remain aware of it throughout the entire process, even if you can't label it. This feeling will inform every design decision you make, especially the colors you choose.

Contrast

There's no excuse for boring color. I'd rather see *bad* color than boring color: it at least piques my interest by its audacity!

The remedy for boring is simple: *contrast*. In my color classes we repeat this mantra in unison: "A strong color scheme must have contrast."

What I mean is to use contrast in any of the four properties just discussed:

Value. Use contrast among your dark and light colors. If your palette is primarily dark, add an accent of a lighter color. It need not be the lightest color on the wheel. Sometimes interesting contrast can be created by using a value just a couple of shades lighter.

Hue. Use two or more colors. You don't need many colors to make beauty; a palette of two or three colors can have more presence and beauty than one having eight or 12 hues.

Intensity. Splash a saturated, pure color among your palette of low-intensity tones. If your color scheme consists of bright, pure colors, try introducing some muted colors.

Temperature. Watch your color scheme come to life when you combine cool and warm colors.

Just as you build contrast into your designs (see Chapter 1, Unity), you must create contrast in your color palettes. A calculated amount of contrast among palette members makes an exciting color scheme.

The Ever-Inspiring Color Wheel

Color wheels are fantastic, fun (how I love spinning them!) tools that inspire and inform. I use mine regularly—all five of them! You needn't be intimidated by all the extra wedges you previously didn't understand. You now understand hue and intensity (which are shown on most wheels).

The color wheel's greatest value is its presentation of reliable harmonies based on geometric formulas, such as triangles, squares, and rectangles. Use these harmonies as launchpads. Design palettes based on the geometric, tweak and substitute as you like, and watch your color schemes soar.

Also, consulting the wheel keeps your mind open to possibilities beyond your habitual combinations (yes, we all have them). We'll briefly skim four major color schemes. Extensive information about each of them (and more color schemes) is available online or in my book *The Beader's Guide to Color*.

Figure 6-10   The visually striking contrast of cool and warm colors gives this necklace an electric force.

Kristy Nijenkamp
Fiesta, 2008
48 cm long
Lampworked and onyx beads, memory wire; knotting, stringing

Monochromatic

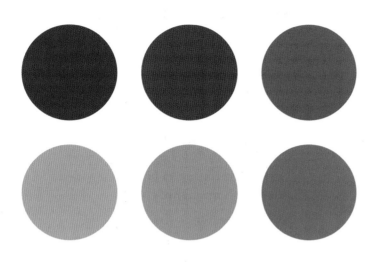

The Monochromatic Palette

Monochromatic palettes consist of one hue. But that doesn't mean they contain only one color. The best monochromatic palettes have a good deal of contrast and a wide range of either value, intensity, or temperature. I've heard people equate monochromatic with boring. This doesn't have to be the case. If your monochromatic palettes are, you've not built in enough contrast. The range of browns in this necklace (figure 6-11) is full of contrast; it forms a beautiful color palette.

When different values, intensities, and temperatures of a hue are combined, gorgeous and evocative harmonies emerge.

If brown is the star of your monochromatic scheme, aim for a variety of browns with different color properties. Expand your palette further by contrasting the bead finishes, combining matte with opaque, ceylon, and transparent finishes, as Jamie Cloud Eakin does in her monochromatic brown necklace (figure 6-11).

Monochromatic palettes are easy to work with, thus a great place to begin if you're color-timid or suffer from bouts of hyperchromacombinia (see page 96). When you consciously create contrast among all the members of your one-hued palette, you'll conjure magnificent monochromatism.

Figure 6-11   This is essentially a monochromatic palette. What makes it exciting is its wide range of value, varying color temperatures, and several different bead surface finishes.

Jamie Cloud Eakin
Untitled, 2008
38 x 7.6 x 1.3 cm
Wood, picture jasper, green/brown jasper, mocha mint jasper, Czech glass, freshwater pearls, crystal, brown agate; bead embroidery

Analogous

The Analogous Palette

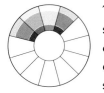 The word analogy means "a similarity between like features of two things." Analogous colors are similar. Analogous schemes involve two or more colors that sit next to each other on the wheel, including pure hues, light and dark versions of hues, and various intensities and temperatures.

Because they are so alike, analogous colors swirl and flow into one another, defying boundaries. You'll find them everywhere in nature: sunsets that fade from pink to orange, rose petals that are yellow at their center and deep crimson at their tips, and bird wings shifting from blue to teal to green.

The emotional impact of analogous palettes is tremendous. Because colors are grouped in a specific area of the wheel, they tend toward warm or cool. This gives analogous schemes a definitive mood. Stephanie Sersich's analogous palette occupies the cool side of the color wheel (figure 6-12). Although many colors are possible in an analogous scheme, retain the temperature and overall mood by using four or fewer colors.

Analogous colors are intrinsically harmonious because the hues are similar. Along with mono-chromatic schemes, they're the easiest to harmonize and combine successfully.

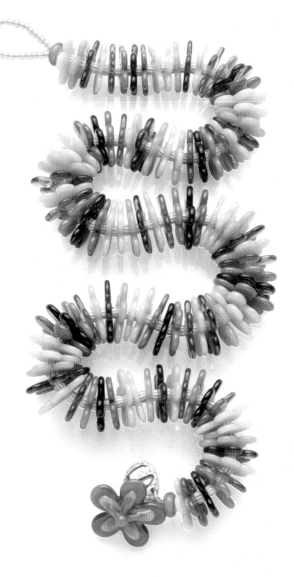

Figure 6-12

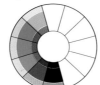

This beautiful analogous palette is exceptionally intriguing because carefully controlled contrast abounds. Look at the range of lights and darks and different glass finishes.

Stephanie Sersich
Flower Necklace, 2010
35 x 5 x 2.5 cm
Handmade glass beads and button, seed beads; strung
PHOTO BY TOM EICHLER

Complementary

The Complementary Palette

Complementary colors sit opposite one another on the wheel. If you aim straight across from yellow, you'll land on violet, yellow's direct complement.

Complements deliver exciting, vibrant harmonies. Understanding their relationships is essential to great use of color. They are the most dynamic of all color contrasts. Complementary colors are least like each other. For example, red is least like green than any hue on the wheel. As you move away from red toward green, the colors are more similar to green, and therefore provide less contrast. Two complementary colors in a palette furnish the most contrast in hue possible—and you know how important contrast is!

Since complementary relationships are chock full of contrast, successful combinations depend entirely on proportions. Too much of one or both complementary colors can collide and pulsate uncomfortably. A reliable approach is to think small: introduce just a whisper of the complement. Used strategically, a tingling sparkle of the dominant color's complement can turn an ordinary palette into an extraordinary delight (figure 6-13).

When your palette is muted, the overall contrast is reduced because the colors are more similar in tone. Therefore you can be more free, less controlled with your complementary proportions. Muted pinks and deep reds combined with complementary yellow-greens in figure 6-14 provide visual dynamism, but are less striking than their brighter, more saturated versions.

Figure 6-13

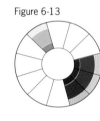

The reds, which lean into purplish maroons, are accented by yellow-green, which lives across the color wheel. Complementary harmonies, whether directly across the wheel or indirect like this one, make attention-getting, exciting color schemes because of the strong contrast of hue and temperature.

Dan Cormier
Botanical Pin, 2005
6 x 6 cm
Polymer clay, sterling silver; Cormier veneer
PHOTO BY ARTIST

Figure 6-14

A palette built on the red-green complement.

Marilyn Parker
Falling Leaves, 2008
71 cm long
Seed beads and garnets; peyote and brick stitch, fringe

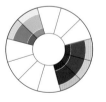

Triadic

Figure 6-15   A complementary triadic scheme

Candace Cloud McLean
Untitled, 2010
55.8 cm
Glass pearls, Czech glass, lampworked glass foil
beads, pewter; stringing, wire work

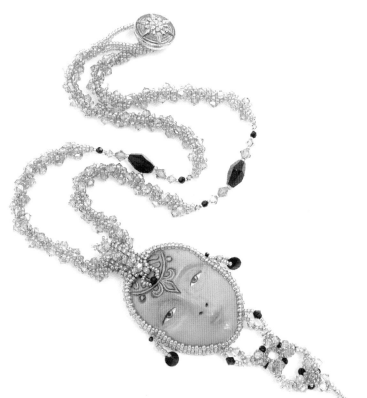

Figure 6-15   A complementary triadic scheme

SaraBeth Cullinan
Untitled, 2008
38.1 x 5 cm
Seed beads, crystals, polymer clay cabochon by
Jen Martin; bead embroidery, peyote stitch, right
angle weave, and spiral rope chain

The Triadic Palette

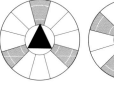

Basic Triad
Every fourth color,
equilateral triangle

Complementary Triad
A pair of
complements and
one between them

Modified Triad
Every other color

Basic triads are composed of three colors equidistant from each other on the color wheel (or every fourth color on the wheel). If counting isn't your thing, locate them by inscribing an equilateral triangle within the wheel.

Triadic combinations exhibit bold, energetic, and striking contrasts in both temperature (warm and cool colors) and value (light and dark colors). Because of its bold directness, the primary triad of the traditional pigment wheel—yellow-red-blue—is often used in children's toys and graphic design.

Complementary triads are formed by combining any two complements with one of the two available colors midway between them. The addition of the third color adds even more contrast to a complementary harmony. In figure 6-15, the third color added to the lime-purple duo is a warm red. Cyan rather than red is used in figure 6-16, making a cooler complementary triad.

Changing the third color brings a dramatic new temperature to a piece. Because the two available accent colors are opposite each other on the wheel, one triad will always be warmer than the other.

Modified triads are created by choosing three colors on the wheel with one space separating them instead of the two spaces used to create complementary triads. Because of this modification, they offer less contrast than complementary triads. They are similar to analogous schemes, but show slightly more contrast. The contrast occurs because the colors at either end of the arc are further apart than a three-color analogous arc.

PROPORTIONS

Shelley Gross asked, "How do you pick out colors that are strikingly different but still look fab together?" The answer—and the magic—lies in the proportions. The more different your colors, the more critical your proportions. A harmonious, memorable palette must be as carefully balanced as a mobile. Yellow and purple (complementary colors) couldn't be more different. A dot of yellow interacts with a dot of purple much differently than it does with an expansive field of purple.

Proportions—how much of one color in relation to another—are the key to what makes a palette sing. When you artfully assign the amount each color occupies within a palette, you'll be able to successfully combine hues of all kinds.

Domination Rules

Though domination is not the recommended means of getting what you want in life, it is encouraged when you want to concoct a head-turning color palette.

When you use equal amounts of each color within a palette you run the risk of creating stasis because often not enough movement or tension will be present. To avoid this, choose a color to dominate the palette (figure 6-16). Let it be the most pronounced, the star, the one everyone sees first and sees the most.

Figure 6-16

One family of color dominates—coral pink— while gold and ivory accents lend quietly effusive sparkles.

Margie Deeb
Woven by Frieda Bates
The Glamour, 2004
80 x 11.4 x 0.5 cm
Sead beads; loom beadweaving
PHOTO BY HAIGWOOD STUDIOS

Figure 6-17
Aquas and teal dominate this palette, while beige is the secondary color. Accents of white add a high note to the scheme.

Marilyn Parker
Sand and Sea, 2009
35 x 28 x 1.5 cm
Seed beads, pearls, turquoise, shells; bead embroidery, embellishment, fringe

Figure 6-18

Margie Deeb
Untitled, 2007
9 x 3 x 0.5 cm
Seed beads, shell, brass; bead embroidery, stringing

Figure 6-19

Inger Marie Berg
Red Cone Necklace,
2009
48.5 cm long
Sterling silver, plastic,
hematite, glass beads;
hand fabricated
PHOTO BY JAN ERIK LANGNES

Figure 6-20

Melanie Moertel
White Islands Bracelet, 2011
21.5 cm long
Lampworked beads, silk ribbon,
sterling silver
PHOTO BY ARTIST

Figure 6-21

Beverly Ash Gilbert
Undersea Volcano, 2009
50.8 x 17.8 x 1.3 cm
Seed beads, gems, glass
beads, buttons; freeform
beadweaving
PHOTO BY ARTIST

Rather than one color dominating the palette, consider using a range of colors (e.g., blues and greens) or a family of colors (e.g., high intensity colors) as a dominant force.

When planning proportions, think in terms of a dominant color (or range of colors); a secondary color (or range of colors); and an accent color or colors, as Marilyn Parker has done (figure 6-17). I'm not restricting your palettes to three colors. A family of colors, or range of hues can dominate, like the palette of the earrings in figure 6-18. Ten variations of green dominate, with an accent of five fucshia/magenta variations.

Red dominates while black forms the secondary color in Inger Marie Berg's necklace (figure 6-19). Because of the vibrant morsels of electric yellow-green accents, the whole piece comes to life like a bioluminescent sea creature.

Karen Reshetar asks, "How do you balance the colors you use? I read to use 60% of your main color, 30% of your secondary color, with a 10% accent. Is that a good rule of thumb?"

No formula will work for every palette; however, this 60-30-10 formula is a valuable springboard for experimentation. The more space your dominant color occupies, the more powerful the palette. I often let the dominant color family occupy 70% or more of the palette. This amount firmly establishes the expressive emotional theme the dominant color conveys, while allowing other colors to support it. Compare the impact red has in figures 6-19, 6-20, and 6-21. When it dominates the palette, red is forceful, bold, and commanding. When used strategically as an accent in 6-20, red is more seductive, flirtatious, and compelling rather than forceful. When used as a focal color surrounded by other strong colors (figure 6-21), it commands attention but doesn't eclipse the other palette members.

Unity through Color Dominance

As stated in Chapter 1, a sense of unity is inherent in well-designed jewelry. Try using color as your unifying element. It can be the most reliable, powerful, and simplest method, as you can see on these two pages. All of the examples shown are strongly unified through color.

THE TONAL APPROACH

Rather than specific hues, the tonal approach to color palettes uses colors within a defined range of saturation as the dominant force. Think of it as painting with a prescribed range of tones. This method asks that we be keenly aware of the nuances of intensity more than hue or even value, though value continues to play a critical role. Because each tonal family shares a similar saturation, pleasing harmonies are relatively easy to achieve. As with all approaches, be sure to include enough contrast to make the palette interesting.

In each example on this page no single color dominates. The piece is unified by the level of intensity the colors share.

Margie Deeb
Untitled, 2007
Czech pressed glass;
stringing

Pastel Tints are hues that have been lightened with white. When used as a group of colors, they're referred to as pastel colors. They combine effortlessly together. Be aware, however, that a pastel palette is given to being overly sweet or passive. Create a memorable palette by including an array of dark and light values. Value contrast gives a pastel palette the vitality it needs.

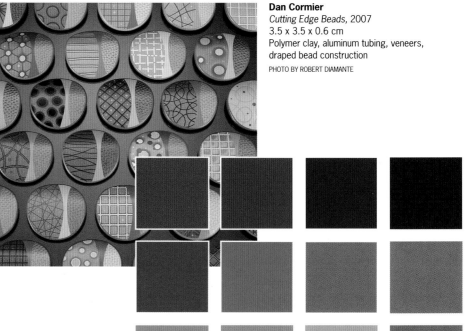

Dan Cormier
Cutting Edge Beads, 2007
3.5 x 3.5 x 0.6 cm
Polymer clay, aluminum tubing, veneers,
draped bead construction
PHOTO BY ROBERT DIAMANTE

Margie Deeb
Woven by Frieda Bates
High Priestess, 2007
80 x 11.4 x 0.5 cm
Cylinder beads, Czech crystals;
loom weavingw

Muted Tones are complex colors comprised of mixtures of hues. They vary in their degree of saturation, some muted to the point of being almost neutral. Sophisticated and sometimes unusual, they suggest conservative refinement and elegance.

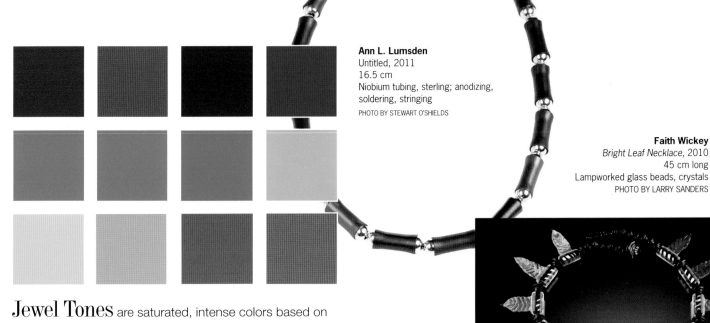

Ann L. Lumsden
Untitled, 2011
16.5 cm
Niobium tubing, sterling; anodizing, soldering, stringing
PHOTO BY STEWART O'SHIELDS

Faith Wickey
Bright Leaf Necklace, 2010
45 cm long
Lampworked glass beads, crystals
PHOTO BY LARRY SANDERS

Jewel Tones are saturated, intense colors based on gems (think rubies, emeralds, sapphires, topaz) and semi-precious stones. They present us with drama, flair, and force. Take liberties with this family by including all kinds of vivid colors like pure magenta, fire orange, and acidic lime-green.

Barbara Becker Simon
Peaches in Regalia, 2004
50.8 cm long
Lampworked glass beads, fine silver beads, sterling silver, freshwater pearls
PHOTO BY LARRY SANDERS

Carmen Anderson
Konjo Fikir (Amharic for "Beautiful Love"), 2005
91.4 x 2.2 x 2.4 cm
Polymer clay and hemp beads (hand crafted by artist), brass findings, Ethiopian engagement pendant, leather; stringing
PHOTO BY ROBERT DIAMANTE

Neutral Tones include grays born of black and white, as well as "chromatic neutrals," tones filled with muted color like browns, beiges, and earthy natural tones. Think of neutrals as muted tones taken to the far end of low saturation.

105

SKIN TONE & COLOR

On page 94 in the intensity section, we explored how some colors come alive when positioned next to others. Likewise, when you match the colors you wear to your skin's undertones, there's a visual reaction. Your skin glows, appearing more radiant. Your eyes appear brighter. Even your hair appears to reflect more highlights.

We've been told to wear colors compatible with our basic coloring. What a confusing and a highly subjective topic! Several complex systems have been devised to pinpoint your compatible colors. Some are very valuable and worth learning. For our purposes in these pages, however, I offer you a basic, simple approach that works and doesn't require years of study. Keep in mind that what matters most—far more than how you think you look—is how you feel in the colors you wear. I look great in chocolate brown, but I can't bear to wear it. I don't resonate with it. If you feel more alive and vibrant in a particular color, wear it! And don't forget to consider clients' skin tone when choosing colors for custom designs.

Undertones: Warm, Neutral & Cool

Flesh has warm, neutral, or cool undertones. Unless you are very pale or very dark, the vein test is an easy way to determine your skin tone. In natural light, during the day, stand by an open window, make a fist and examine your inner wrist. If your veins appear:

- green: you are probably warm toned

- mix of blue and green: you are probably neutral toned.

- blue: you are probably cool toned

If you can't discern vein color, hold white paper or a white towel up against your skin in natural light. Is it more yellow (warm) or pink (cool)?

This can be tricky. Even pale ruddy skin can be more honey-toned than pink. It is best to do this with a friend and compare what you both are seeing. Or ask for help at a makeup counter.

WARM

Warm-toned skin:
- golden, yellow, or apricot undertones

- hair tends to have hints of orange, yellow, red, or gold

- eye color tends to be amber, dark brown, hazel, or dark green

Looks most alive and vibrant wearing:
- gold, warm, or brass-toned metals

- yellow-based and earthy colors: oranges, bronzes, golds, peaches, brick reds, earthy greens, mocha browns, ivory

Avoid:
- large expanses of black; if worn too close to the face it can make the face look washed out

NEUTRAL

Neutral-toned skin:
- the best of both warm and cool-toned skin

Neutral-toned people can wear many colors in many tones and look great.

Some neutral skin tones lean toward either warm or cool. When they lean toward warm, they look best in warm colors with golden undertones, but can wear cool palettes. Follow the warm-toned guidelines.

When they lean toward cool, they look best in cool colors with pink or blue undertones, but can wear warm palettes. Follow the cool-toned guidelines.

COOL

Cool-toned skin:
- pink or rosy undertone

- hair often contains blue, blue-violet, silver, ash undertones

- eye color tends to be blue, gray-green, gray-blue, blue green, or green

Looks most alive and vibrant wearing:
- silver, platinum, and pewter metals

- blue-based colors: jewel tones, royal or icy blues, rosy pinks, silvers, plums, pure white, light pinks, true reds

- can easily wear black

Avoid:
- oranges, golds, beige

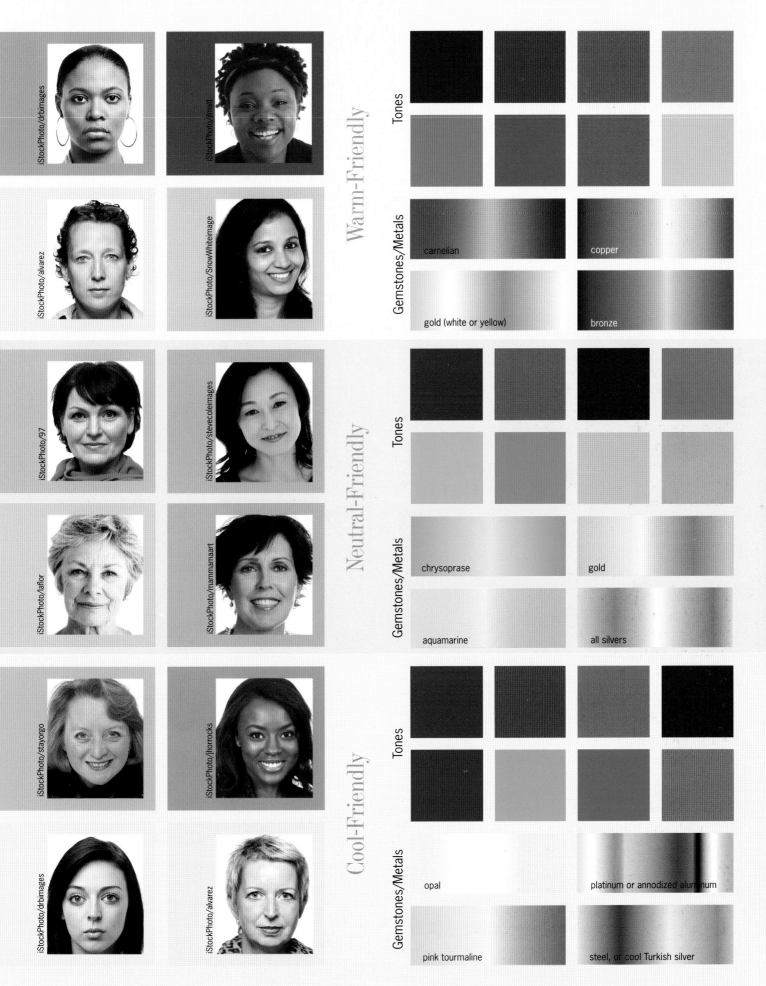

Warm-Friendly

Tones

Gemstones/Metals

carnelian   copper

gold (white or yellow)   bronze

Neutral-Friendly

Tones

Gemstones/Metals

chrysoprase   gold

aquamarine   all silvers

Cool-Friendly

Tones

Gemstones/Metals

opal   platinum or annodized aluminum

pink tourmaline   steel, or cool Turkish silver

iStockPhoto/drbimages
iStockPhoto/jfmatt
iStockPhoto/alvarez
iStockPhoto/SnowWhiteimage
iStockPhoto/97
iStockPhoto/stevecoleimages
iStockPhoto/laflor
iStockPhoto/mammamaart
iStockPhoto/stayorgo
iStockPhoto/horrocks
iStockPhoto/drbimages
iStockPhoto/alvarez

Color Study

USING HER LAMPWORKED BEAD floral bracelet design, Marcy Lamberson and I explored the four tonal families described on pages 104–105. As stated earlier, when you work with colors within a specific zone of saturation, as Marcy did in each of the bracelets below, making a unified, harmonious palette becomes relatively easy. Though it's important to remain mindful of proportions, they are less critical when approaching color this way. Marcy not only worked within tonal families, but also limited her palettes to two or selections, creating evocative and strong color harmonies.

Marcy Lamberson
Wristy Business (four floral versions), 2012
Each 22.2 x 3 x 2 cm
Lampworked glass beads by artist, crystals, glass pearls, seed beads, sterling, memory wire

Pastel Tints
Marcy created an enduring pastel palette by including an array of lights and darks, not just soft tints, like most pastel palettes tend to be. The blue stands out. The green in the lampworked beads is a medium value and in the strand it is much lighter. Far from demure, the bicones in the strand offer a flare of pink. At this level of saturation pink could overthrow the rest of the palette, but it doesn't because at 4 mm, these bicones are so small.

Jewel Tones
To augment the jewel tones, Marcy used mostly transparent glass, which conveys a rich and sparkling luxury. She limited her hues to a range of blues and greens, keeping the overall temperature cool. The result is a robust palette singing with gorgeous color.

Muted Tones
Complex colors often suggest conservative sophistication. This isn't the peppy palette of spring, like the pastel scheme above. It is more mature, taking its time to offer up a statement of refined elegance. As balanced as it is beautiful, just two colors, green and mauve, bring peace and grace.

Neutral Tones
Here Marcy has created one of the liveliest neutral palettes I've ever seen. The beads are full of texture and activity. Limiting the palette to neutrals keeps it from becoming overly noisy or busy. The dots, being much lighter than the other colors, add a playful energy.

Challenge Yourself

1

Property Study

Make three pieces of jewelry. In each, focus on contrasting one of these properties:

Value contrast: Use a very light color (or colors) and a very dark color (or colors).

Intensity contrast: Use a saturated color (or colors) and one or two muted, dull colors.

Temperature contrast: Use a warm color (or group of colors) and one very cool color.

In all three pieces, pay conscious attention to balancing the proportions of each property.

2

Tonal Study

Make a simple piece of jewelry and repeat it in the four tonal palettes presented on pages 104–105: pastel, muted, jewel, and neutral tones. Color is frequency: Be as aware as possible of the energy of each palette as you work. Try to get to know each family of tones intimately, especially if it is one you are unfamiliar with.

3

Palette Study

Choose two pieces of jewelry, one whose palette you consider boring, the other whose palette you consider lively. The selections can be photos of jewelry, or your own pieces. Examine them for the following:

• Is color contrast present? If so, what kind of contrast: value, hue, intensity, temperature?

• Is there enough contrast, too much, or not enough for your taste?

• Is there a dominant force, either a color, color family, or dominant group of colors?

• What kinds of colors are used—light or dark, saturated or muted, warm or cool? Is there an overall light/dark, saturated/muted, warm/cool tone to each piece?

• What makes the boring piece boring?

• What makes the dynamic piece lively?

Now that you've examined the two pieces of jewelry, how will you incorporate what you've learned into your own work?

7 | Jewelry & The Body

As a designer, I want my jewelry to make the woman wearing it feel her beauty. When fringe drapes from my earlobes and brushes my shoulders I'm aware of my sensuality, which makes me feel more alive and happy. When I sparkle with color, I'm more engaged with life. Sensuality, aliveness, happiness, and presence are part of my beauty, part of everyone's beauty. When one of us feels alive with our beauty, there is more beauty in the world.

Our bodies vary in shape, size, and proportions, presenting a diverse array of canvases on which our jewelry will be displayed. And each one of those presents visual and artistic challenges.

In this chapter we'll learn to emphasize and de-emphasize specific areas of the body to enhance its beauty. Like magicians, we'll divert attention away from one place and lead it directly to another. After we've studied these concepts, I'll close by giving you a chart for recording all the necessary information to create beautiful, personalized jewelry for your customers. Consider this just one of the gifts you offer the world: helping each person, including yourself, get more in touch with their beauty.

Figure 7-1   **Jamie Cloud Eakin**
Lady in the Forest, 2012
34 cm long; pendant 5 x 10 cm
Aventurine, brass button, tiger eye, green and brown jasper; bead embroidery, branch fringe

MOVING WITH THE BODY

Just as clothing must move with the body, so must jewelry. How irritating are jeans so stiff that they don't twist when you do? You turn right while the waistband continues to face left. And the knees retain their folds while you stand. Not fun. Not attractive.

I've seen the above scenario in some large bead-embroidered bib necklaces. If you're a designer caught up in the gravitational pull of this style, remember that a necklace needs to be supple enough to conform to and move with the body. Wearing a stiff necklace isn't pleasant, no matter how stunning the design. It may appear lovely in a photograph, but can it be worn without inducing discomfort? And does it achieve the goal of making the wearer feel more beautiful?

The first step to making comfortable jewelry that moves with the body is to test-drive your piece before you wear, give, or sell it. Make sure you like how it feels and moves. If not, make changes. Use a lighter, more supple backing, add extra jump rings at junctions, smooth out burrs that poke, re-string. Do whatever you need to do to make your jewelry a pleasure to wear.

The chart below suggests solutions to common problems.

MOVEMENT PROBLEMS	POSSIBLE SOLUTIONS
A bracelet slides and its clasp sits on the top of the wrist	• add a counterweight to balance the piece • make sure the clasp is as heavy as the front of the bracelet • intentionally design the components and clasp similar in weight and appearance so the bracelet can be rotated and looks good from every angle
The necklace slides and its clasp lands in the front	• consider adding a counterweight in back to balance the piece • lighten the back half of the necklace so the majority of the weight is positioned in front
Necklace strands are strung so tightly the strand doesn't drape	• lay the necklace out straight, remove beads to add space so gentle tension is present, curve into a circle, secure the tension, then crimp or tie off
Necklace strands are so heavy they pull on the neck uncomfortably	• if you can't lighten the load by shortening, consider distributing the weight among a wider area, maybe using more strands • use a multistrand clasp that acts as a flat, multilayered cushion on the back of the neck • use separator bars 1 or 2 inches (2.5–5 cm) away from the clasp
Earrings are too heavy	• use posts instead of wire hooks so the earring fits more snugly against the lobe, thus reducing movement and distributing weight • with posts, use earring nuts with large flat side to sandwich the lobe securely and help the earring hang better • use lighter materials: consider hollow glass beads, acrylic, Lucite, wood, and plastic when making huge earrings
Bead embroidered bib necklace is too stiff	• use lighter, more supple backing and interfacing • stitch less tightly, more uniform and loose • rely on beaded bezels rather than glue to secure stones to the foundation • build curves into necklaces by creating them on a form or mannequin rather than on a flat surface

Aside from the knowledge of technique, a jewelry designer must have a reverence for beauty: the beauty of form and the beauty of the human body. This reverence informs how you'll handle the interplay between jewelry, clothing, and the body. Unless you're designing for a mannequin in a photo, you must consider these interactions. They are critical to overall aesthetics.

I hear you thinking, "Oh no, a set of rules!" These aren't rules. They're general guidelines to help you design the most flattering

A Little Breathing Room: Necklace to Neckline Distance

Don't let the necklace touch or ride along the neckline. This creates competition between necklace and neckline, diminishing the beauty of both. Also, the necklace doesn't wear properly: it slips inside and outside of the garment when the wearer moves, creating discomfort.

Leave at least 1 inch (2.5 cm) between necklace and neckline.

Unintentional Shapes

Be aware of shapes formed by the spaces between the sides of the necklace and the neckline. These can be awkward and confusing, and distract from the beauty of the necklace and it's wearer.

In most cases, the goal is to mirror the shape of the neckline and softly frame the neck.

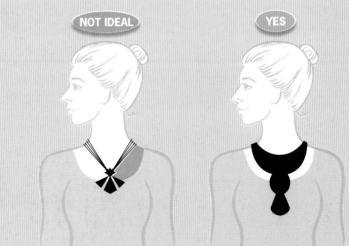

When layering several necklaces of unequal length, aim for equal spacing, or pleasing proportions between them.

styles for yourself and your customer's face, neckline, and clothing. When doing custom work, you need to consult with your clients to ensure you're making jewelry that enhances not only their wardrobe, but their proportions and lifestyle. See the Customer Preference form on pages 128-129 for more.

As valuable as they are, style guidelines are only part of the picture. How we look in a piece of jewelry hinges on how we relate to people and our world. Our attitude contributes more to our appearance than any fashion protocol.

Large Bustlines

Large bustlines naturally draw attention. Whether you want to draw even more attention with jewelry is your choice. If you do, I suggest you use subtlety. Let your focal bead or pendant land at least 1 inch (2.5 cm) above the cleavage. Allow strands to fall well below the bustline, or to the waistline to emphasize the thinner part of the torso. Consider the following:

• avoid necklaces and pendants which get stuck in the cleavage—this look doesn't do the girls any favors

• avoid necklaces and pendants that dangle, as if off the edge of a cliff, from the bustline

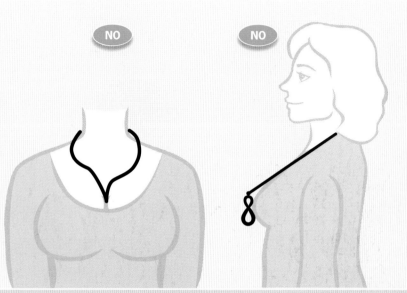

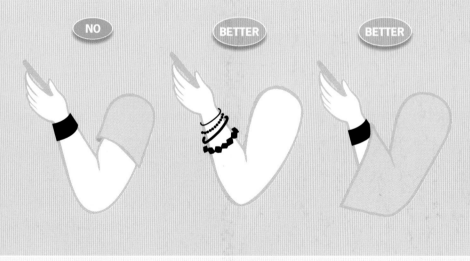

Thick Arms & Hands

Cuff bracelets make thick arms and hands look heavier. Tips to mitigate this:

• avoid wearing wide cuffs with short sleeves that section the arm horizontally

• many thin bracelets add less visual weight than one solid cuff

• push cuff as far from hand as possible

• bell, long, or three-quarter sleeves look best when wearing wide bracelets

• avoid tight-fitting bracelets

Crew Neck T-shirts

A beautiful hand-crafted necklace worn on a crew neck T-shirt doesn't do your jewelry any favors. Much more flattering—and just as comfy— are round and scoop-necked T's in all colors and sizes.

JEWEL

Jewel necklines work well with most necklace shapes, styles, and lengths, as long as the necklace falls below the curve, or fully covers the curve, creating its own neckline. Fill the chest area with jewelry!

V-NECK

The flattering V-neck supports most necklace styles. Work with the V to draw the eye up and down. Follow the V shape, don't try to compete with it.

BATEAU/ SABRINA

Think "contrast" when designing for these elegant necklines. Counter the strong horizontal line with strong verticals or soft curves. Create vertical interest. This neckline draws attention to large shoulders and bustline.

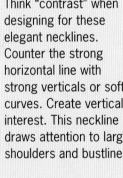

COWL

Create an elegant, flattering look by wearing long necklaces, multistrands, and bold styles worn tucked beneath the cowl. This is a great neckline for big linked chains and long strands of large, chunky stones.

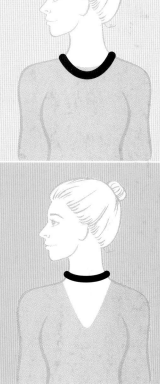

Avoid shapes that fall directly on the curve of the neckline, as this competes with it.

Avoid chokers that draw attention up and create an odd gap between neckline and necklace, making the neck appear thicker.

If you echo the V-shape, avoid doing so directly along the neckline. Allow 1 inch (2.5 cm) between necklace and neckline.

Because this neckline draws attention to large shoulders and bustline, avoid overemphasizing the horizontal.

Avoid a length that ends right at the collar.

Avoid necklaces hanging on top of the cowl.

Avoid short pieces that appear to choke the wearer.

When the necklace is touching or too close to the cowl, the result is bulky and cumbersome.

TURTLE

The neck area is occupied, so let the jewelry hang lower, filling the chest area. The turtleneck creates an abrupt horizontal line. Soften it with either curves or length. Draw the eye up and down.

SQUARE

Fill the space the square neckline affords with layered chains, horizontal styles, and bibs. If you want to soften the angles use curves and organic shapes. For an edgier look, emphasize the angles by wearing geometric shapes.

SCOOP

The scoop—or round—neckline is easy to wear necklaces with because it flatters any neck and leaves room for most necklace shapes. The best look is to mirror the shape of the neckline and softly frame the neck.

SWEETHEART/QUEEN ANNE

These necklines are beautifully feminine. Most necklace shapes work as long as they don't obscure the silhouette of the neckline. Choose a necklace that doesn't touch the bottom of the neckline.

Avoid short chains and pendants; they produce a tight, choked look.

Avoid tucking the chain inside the funnel and allowing the pendant to drop just below it.

Avoid overwhelming or obscuring the shape of the neckline.

Be mindful of the shapes created by exposed skin. Be sure they are not distracting.

Be mindful of proportions: avoid too much space between sides of neckline and necklace.

Avoid a pendant that sits on the neckline.

Avoid heavy pendants that pull the necklace into a V-shape.

Avoid overpowering or obscuring the elegant, feminine shape of the neckline with a necklace that's too dramatic or busy.

Make sure that the shapes created by exposed skin are not distracting.

Body *scale* must be considered when designing. The scale of the jewelry should be proportionate to physical size. Determine body scale by factoring in bone structure (the size of wrists and ankles), the size of facial features, and the amount of space your customer's body appears to occupy. Larger jewelry works best on larger women; smaller jewelry works best on smaller women. Below are basic guidelines to help you make the most flattering jewelry for specific body frames and heights.

PETITE

6' (183 cm)
5' (152 cm)
4' (122 cm)

Petite body types need to achieve a balance of body frame and volume of accessories. Whether heavy or thin, it's important not to overwhelm the petite woman with large, bulky accessories that make her appear as if she's drowning in jewelry. Jewelry with a more open look (chains and strands with spaces between beads) is preferable to solid, thick masses.

As with all heights, if bone structure is large, or the woman is heavier, she can wear more solid, chunky, striking jewelry. In these cases, prominent jewelry is more proportionate and has a balancing, slimming effect.

NO

YES

iStockPhoto/drbimages

MEDIUM

Medium height is considered between 5'5" and 5'7" (165–170 cm).

Where you choose to draw attention depends on body proportions and what you want to emphasize. If the torso is long and the legs are short, draw the observer's eye up toward the shoulders and face.

If the legs are longer than the torso, wear medium-long to long accessories to draw attention down.

As with all heights, if bone structure is large, chunkier, bolder jewelry can be appropriate and can provide balance and proportion.

YES FOR LONG TORSO

YES FOR LONG LEGS

iStockPhoto/drbimages

TALL

Bold jewelry is a natural fit for women over 5'7" (170 cm). Given their commanding presence, tall women can wear accessories with substance, like statement bracelets (or lots of bangles), and unusual, one-of-a-kind focal beads. If it doesn't make a statement, jewelry can get lost on a tall woman.

Avoid dainty chains and delicate romantic, filigree jewelry.

As with all heights, this formula works: the larger the bone structure, the more striking the jewelry. Remember that prominent jewelry can balance large bone structure and create a slimming effect.

NO

YES

iStockPhoto/drbimages

Because of our different frames and shapes, weight lands in different areas. Here are basic jewelry guidelines for de-emphasizing bulk and flattering the curves.

Large Bust, Minimal Waist

- slim the waist as much as possible

- reduce bulk and visual activity around the bustline

- don't thicken the neck

The necklace falls too close to the bustline, creating horizontal emphasis; large chunky shapes in the chest area add too much bulk.

Multiple long strands and focal points draw the eye vertically. Be careful: multiple pendant focal points may add a bit too much bulk.

The open area around the neck allows the face to shine, the pendant falls below the bustline, and the tassels fall below the waistline, balancing the proportions.

iStockPhoto/ drbimages

iStockPhoto/ AndreasReh

Large Bust and Hips, Defined Waist

- emphasize the waist

- don't add bulk around the bustline

- don't draw extra attention to the bustline

- don't thicken the neck

The necklace falls at the bustline, creating horizontal emphasis.

This short necklace falls well above the bustline and far enough below the chin to slenderize the neck. Its lush texture brings attention up and away from the bustline.

Multiple elegant strands create vertical emphasis and draw attention to the waistline.

FLATTERING THE NECK

The neck is the canvas for the necklace. Long, short, wide, thin, smooth, or wrinkled, our necks deserve to be adorned, for they work long and hard all day. And they are beautiful. Let's consider how to honor their beauty with flattering styles.

Long & Thin Neck

- wear soft, round necklaces

- wear many strands with the shortest strand hugging the base of the neck

- wear round earrings, and earrings with round components and motifs

- large choker-style necklaces look great on long necks

- avoid styles that lengthen the neck (unless you want to lengthen it further), such as V-shaped necklaces or heavy pendants which pull the necklace into a V.

iStockPhoto/Yuri Arcurs

Short & Thick Neck

- wear large chains and necklaces that begin 2 inches (5 cm) below the collarbone

- long, graduated necklaces are flattering— 18 to 24 inches (45 to 61 cm) in length

- wear V-shaped pendants that hang well below the collarbone and draw attention downward

- wear long earrings and dangles that visually lengthen the neck

- avoid short, thick necklaces or anything that fits close to the neck

iStockPhoto/drbimages

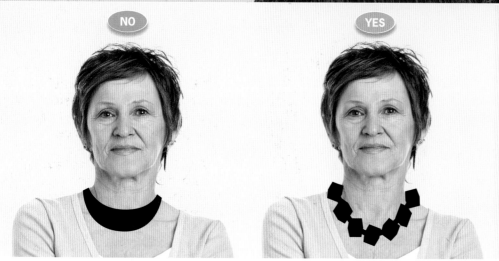

Soft & Fleshy Neck

- create a counterpoint to soft folds by wearing angular pendants, geometric shapes and motifs

- avoid short, thick necklaces which accentuate width

- avoid anything that fits close to the neck

iStockPhoto/drbimages

The rule of thumb for wearing glasses is: the more prominent the glasses, the more carefully you need to balance the jewelry. Hair must also be considered. Hairstyles with lots of texture, large or striking shape, stark highlights, and unusual color add another visually competing element. Without discretion, the look can overwhelm the face. My personal guideline is to wear what enhances the face. If you've overwhelmed the face, you've got too much going on.

Visually Dominant Glasses   **Visually Subdued Glasses**

LEFT Large, intricate, moving earrings compete with prominent glassses and with lots of abundantly textured hair.

Curly, thick, full hair, like the style illustrated here, can be considered an accessory.

RIGHT Bring down the volume on just one item, in this case the glasses, and the overall effect is much easier on the eyes.

LEFT These earrings are simpler than the ones above, and harmonize better with the very dominant glasses.

RIGHT This shows more visual balance among hair, glasses, and jewelry.

LEFT Shorter, less textured, smoother hair affords dramatic earrings the space to work their magic. No visual chaos here.

RIGHT Circles are echoed and repeated in the eyeglass lenses and the earrings, creating visual harmony.

OBLONG & RECTANGLE

I'm fascinated by facial differences that are deemed "disproportionate" or "unappealing": an extra large nose, for example, eyes that tilt upwards at the outer edges, or distinctive wrinkles that tell of a life well lived. I enjoy drawing, painting, and making jewelry for faces that are unusual precisely because of their uniqueness, because they are not average. Our challenge as jewelry designers is to find ways to flatter every shape.

There are, however, preferences humans have for what is considered visually pleasing. (Obviously, these have nothing to do with a person's true beauty.)

If you combine all the faces of Western culture to form a single, composite image, you'll get the oval shape, which is considered the average among our population. Culturally, people find faces that approximate its average face to be the most attractive. Therefore, the oval-shaped face is considered the most attractive in our culture. It is also the most common, and considered the most versatile. Many different hairstyles, eyeglasses, necklines, and earrings flatter the oval shaped face.

We each have a unique face with a unique length-to-width ratio, jaw, jaw-line, and front-on outline. All faces don't fit neatly into the categories we're going to discuss on the next few pages. Certified professional image consultant Jane Liddelow (www.style-makeover-hq.com) explains: "...if your face length is definitely longer than wide and you have a broad, square jaw-line then your face shape falls into the rectangle

- face is longer than wide
- forehead, cheekbones, and jaw line are the same width
- hairline may be rounded
- sides of face are straight

Hair line:

- **oblong** hairline may be rounded
- **rectangular** hairline is most likely straight

Jaw line:

- **oblong** jaw-line is softly rounded;
- **rectangular** jaw is broad and jaw-line is square

category. However, if, when looking at your front-on outline, your jaw is the widest part of your face, the triangle category may be a better choice for you. It'll depend how much longer than wide your face is: do you see your face length first? Or is your jaw more obvious than the length?"

Determining Your Face Shape

If you've struggled to identify your face shape, the easiest way is to have someone take a photo. Or shoot it yourself with your camera phone in a large mirror. Pull your hair back from your face, hold the phone at eye level to the side of your head, parallel to the mirror—don't tilt the phone or your face. And don't stand too close or you'll get a distorted, fish-eye effect. Measure and draw on your printed photo.

Pleasing Earring Shapes

In our quest to frame the face and complement the eyes, certain earring styles are more suited to specific face shapes than others. On pages 124-125 I suggest flattering earring shapes and sizes. Remember, the goal is to emphasize positive features while minimizing weaker ones.

iStockPhoto/alvarez

iStockPhoto/mammamaart

ROUND

- circular, about as wide as it is long
- jaw line round and full
- cheekbones are the widest part and round
- hairline is often round
- chin is usually rounded

iStockPhoto/97

SQUARE

- almost as wide as it is long
- jaw is broad, jaw-line is square and strong
- sides are straight
- forehead, cheekbones, and jaw are the same width
- hairline is often straight

iStockPhoto/laflor

OVAL

- an inverted egg-shape, widest at cheekbones, slightly longer than wide
- forehead broader than jaw
- jaw-line is slightly rounded
- considered the most pleasing shape

iStockPhoto/drbimages

iStockPhoto/drbimages

HEART

- slightly longer than wide
- wide at forehead and cheeks, then tapers to point at chin
- forehead is wider than or same width as cheekbones
- cheeks are often rounded
- jaw is the narrowest part of face
- jawline is long and pointed
- often has a widow's peak

iStockPhoto/stayorgo

	FACE SHAPE	GOAL	WHAT WORKS
OVAL		since any style flatters the oval shape, choose earring styles that fit your lifestyle and personality	• echo the oval shape with with hoops, curves, teardrops • chandeliers bring attention to the entire length and span of face • triangles are especially flattering
ROUND		to create the illusion of a longer, slimmer face, and draw attention vertically	• flowing, vertical, dangly earrings longer than they are wide • pear-shaped drops draw the eye downward • geometric shapes (triangles, squares, rectangles) distract from roundness • angular studs which point down
OBLONG/ RECTANGULAR		to shorten and broaden the appearance of the face and perhaps soften the jaw-line	• earrings wider than long, go for width • round, square, tear-drop, fan shapes • small hoops and large button posts • drops that are no longer than chin • three-dimensional styles • wide chandeliers with activity and drama: space-filling designs that remain above the chin
SQUARE		to create the illusion of a longer face and perhaps soften the jaw-line	• earrings longer than wide • curves and swirled designs • large oval hoops • long narrow shapes, drops, chandeliers • round studs
HEART		add width to chin, and draw attention away from its point; make forehead appear narrower; add width at jaw-line and chin	• earrings wider at bottom than top • design widest part of earring next to the jaw line • teardrops, triangular, or fan-shaped dangles • horizontal motifs • long, thin dangle drops with large, distinctive stones at the bottom

			AVOID
			Avoid overly long earrings that lengthen the oval.
			Avoid things that accentuate width: round shapes, hoops, small studs, and chunky earrings can all make cheeks more prominent
			Avoid long flat dangles.
			Avoid short posts and wide chandeliers; angular chunky styles make face look more square, possibly wider.
			Avoid anything that tapers as it descends, like short heart-shaped dangles. Avoid small button posts and long narrow styles.

STANDARD JEWELRY FITTING AND SIZES

To help design for the varied bodies of your clients, you'll find some standard measurements in the charts here. But always take measurements when possible. Gather and record measurements on the Customer Preference Form (pages 128–129).

Necklaces: When necklace measurements are written, the number includes the entire necklace. For example, a length of 24 inches (61 cm) includes the findings, clasp, and end ring.

Earrings: Viewed from the front, length is from the top of the earring to the bottom edge of the longest bead. Width is the widest part as seen from the front. Depth is the widest part of the earring as viewed from the side.

Bracelets: The length includes the clasp and end ring. Laid flat and viewed from above, the width is the widest part.

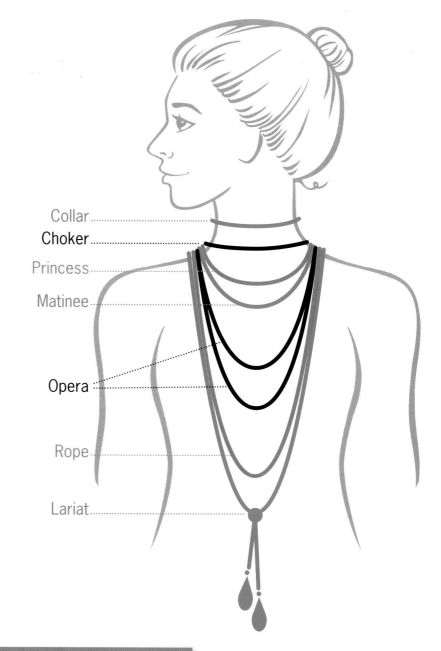

NECKLACES

Name	Description	Length	
		inches	centimeters
Collar	snug fit around middle of neck	12–13″	30–33 cm
Choker	lies around base of neck	14–16″	35–40 cm
Princess	the most popular length, falling just below throat, touching collarbone	17–19″	43–48 cm
Matinee	falls a bit below collarbone	20–24″	51–61 cm
Opera	versatile enough to transform from day to elegant eveningwear, from a double to single strand	28–34″	71–86 cm
Rope	can be doubled to create a multi-strand necklace	over 45″	over 114 cm
Lariat	open-ended, no clasp; often features beads or tassels on ends; versatile, can be worn in many different ways	48″+	122+ cm

You have my permission to photocopy pages 126–127.

BRACELETS

Wrist Measurement		Comfortable Fit		Looser Fit	
inches	centimeters	inches	centimeters	inches	centimeters
5¾" or less	14.6 cm or less	6¾" or less	17 cm or less	7½"	19 cm
6–6¾"	15–17 cm	7–7¾"	17–20 cm	8½"	22 cm
7" or more	17 cm or more	8" or more	20 cm or more	9"	23 cm

Note: When large beads are used the bracelet must be lengthened more (sometimes as much as 1 inch or 2.5 cm) to accommodate the depth of the beads.

Measuring for a Bracelet

Standard bracelet lengths range from 6 to 8 inches (15.2–20.3 cm).

Measure the wrist using flexible tape, a strip of paper, or string. Wrap it completely and comfortably around the wrist. Make the bracelet ¾- to 1 inch (2–2.5 cm) longer than the measurement.

ANKLETS

Anklets are usually 10 inches (25.4 cm) long.

RINGS

Size	Circumference	
	inches	millimeters
0	1.44	36.5
1	1.54	39.1
2	1.64	41.6
3	1.74	44.2
4	1.84	46.7
5	1.94	49.3
6	2.04	51.8
7	2.14	54.4
8	2.24	56.9
9	2.34	59.5
10	2.44	62.1
11	2.54	64.6
12	2.64	67.2
13	2.74	69.7
14	2.85	72.3
15	2.95	74.8
16	3.05	77.4

Note: Fingers swell throughout the day. Therefore, measuring for ring size is best done in warm temperatures at the end of the day.

If the knuckle is larger than the base of the finger, measure both the base of the finger and the knuckle. Choose the size between the two measurements.

If you're making a wide band, make it one size larger than the wearer's measurement so it will be comfortable.

The ring size of the wearer's primary hand will be about a half-size larger than the other.

If the measurement is between two sizes on the chart, use the larger measurement.

Marcy Lamberson
Assorted Rings, 2013
Smallest: 1.5 x 1.5 x 3 cm
Largest: 3.5 x 3.5 x 3 cm
Soft glass, base metal, silver sculptural glass techniques

Measuring for a Ring

To measure ring size, wrap a string around finger.

Mark where the end of the string touches itself. Make sure you've wrapped exactly one time.

Measure the length from the end of string to the mark.

Compare that length to the chart to find your ring size.

CUSTOMER PREFERENCE FORM

Color Preferences

Color Families	Yes	No	Maybe
Pastels			
Brights			
Jewel Tones			
Muted Tones			

Specific Color Likes: _____

_____

Dislikes: _____

_____

Garment Specifics

If you're designing for specific clothing, gather the following information. Take photos of client wearing the garment, and close-ups of garment fabric and color. Try to use natural lighting.

Garment Colors: _____

_____

Fabric Type: _____

Neckline Type: _____

Jewelry Measurements

In addition to measuring the body (see next page), measure customer's existing jewelry.

Desired Earring Length: _____

Desired Necklace Length: _____

Desired Bracelet Length: _____

Ring Finger and Size(s): _____

Metal Preferences

	Yes	No	Maybe
Nickel			
Brass			
Copper			
Vermeil			
Gold			
Sterling Silver			
Surgical Steel			
Niobium			

Finding Preferences

Necklaces/ Bracelets:	Yes	No	Maybe
Toggle			
Lobster			
Magnetic			
Earrings:			
Clips			
Fish Hooks			

Weight of Jewelry

When it comes to weight and volume, what are your clients' preferences? Refer to jewelry they currently wear if necessary.

Earrings: _____

Necklace: _____

Bracelet: _____

Rings: _____

Comfort

Additional relevant issues concerning drape, size, positioning, how the pieces lay on the body, etc.

_____

_____

_____

_____

You have my permission to photocopy pages 128-129.

CUSTOMER MEASUREMENTS FORM

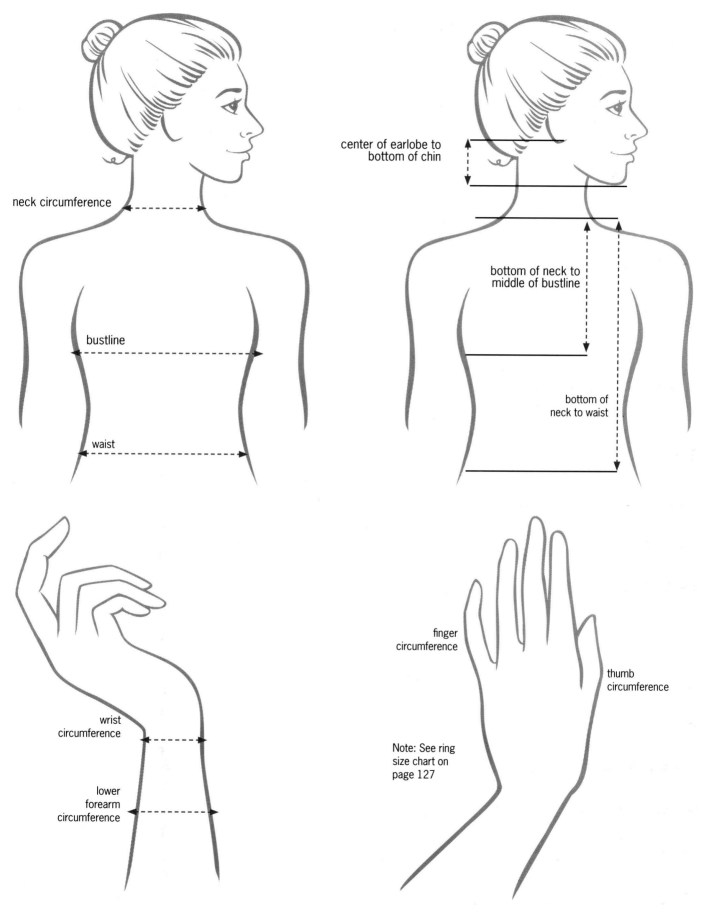

neck circumference

bustline

waist

center of earlobe to bottom of chin

bottom of neck to middle of bustline

bottom of neck to waist

wrist circumference

lower forearm circumference

finger circumference

thumb circumference

Note: See ring size chart on page 127

Write directly on photocopies of this page.

Jewelry on the Body Study

MOST OF THE TIME WE AREN'T designing for the runway, so it's important to look at jewelry on regular women wearing clothing that we wear on a daily basis.

In each photo, decide if the necklace works well with the clothing, and if it complements the woman wearing it. If not, what would you change?

Be sure to consider:

Necklace length
Does it compete with the neckline? Does it lead the eye to an area you think should be accentuated?

Necklace in relation to face and body
Does the volume of the jewelry overwhelm the face? Is the necklace so small as to make the face seem overly large?

Necklace on fabric
If the fabric is printed, does the necklace stand out enough to be seen, or is it visually confusing? If the fabric is a solid color, is there enough contrast for the necklace to be seen, or does it get lost in the fabric?

iStockPhoto/drbimages

iStockPhoto/drbimages

iStockPhoto/ranplett

iStockPhoto/shapecharge

iStockPhoto/laflor

iStockPhoto/Generistock

iStockPhoto/Nadeika

The necklace complements the model: the shape of the beads echoes her eyes—big, round, and adorable.

Challenge Yourself

To familiarize yourself with face and body issues that impact your jewelry designs, answer the questions below on paper. Study photos of yourself to understand what looks best on you and why. The more you understand your own body and how it interacts with jewelry, the more you'll be able to understand the interactions of the body and jewelry on others.

- What type of face do you have? Is it one of those listed on pages 122-123—oval, round, oblong, rectangular, square, heart—or a combination?

- To frame your face and complement your eyes, which earring styles are more suited to your face shape?

- When making earrings for yourself, what techniques will you use to frame your face and complement your eyes?

- How tall are you and what kind of body frame do you have (see page 118)? Does your frame change how you'll design jewelry that flatters your height?

- When you wear necklaces, where do you want to draw attention: your face, eyes, cleavage, waist? What features do you want to emphasize and what do you want to minimize?

Now choose a friend, study her face and body, and answer the questions above.

8 | The Creative Journey

If you've accepted the challenge of this book, you've learned how to fashion your jewelry with harmonious unity. You know how to visually guide someone through your compositions. You can balance, move, shape, and color your jewelry with splendor. Now let's talk about the process: how to get it done.

The most powerful way to become a master at any art form, including jewelry design, is to structure your creative process. Show up regularly, open your heart to wonder, and do your work. When you do your part, the Muse will find all kinds of ways to intervene, showering you with insights, inspiration, and magic.

DAILY PRACTICE & ROUTINE

For me (and every working artist I know), the most important component of process is the routine of daily practice. I keep a regular appointment with my art and I practice like an athlete or performer. The practice of art becomes a discipline which is, for the most part, joyful and invigorating. Over the decades I've purposely established very methodical approaches to my process.

I begin designing jewelry by sketching my ideas upon a rendition of a human form, constantly envisioning how the overall design and the beads will interact with the body (see pages 84–85). It is only after I've

Stephanie Sersich
Spinny Brooch, 2010
4.5 x 4.3 x 2.5 cm
Handmade glass
cabochon, silver findings
PHOTO BY TOM EICHLER

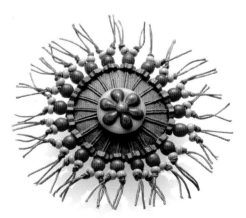

Stephanie Sersich
Mandala Brooch, 2010
8 x 8 x 3.5 cm
Handmade glass
button, glass and
ceramic beads, waxed
linen, silver findings;
knotted
PHOTO BY TOM EICHLER

Carmen Anderson
Tropical Blossoms, 2008
61 cm
Handmade polymer clay beads, glass beads, nylon thread
PHOTO BY ROBERT DIAMANTE

firmed up decisions about size, shape, drape, color, and composition that I seriously consider stitching and technique. When necessary, I bead prototypes and weave color samples.

My unglamorous methods are far removed from the fantasy vision of the artist who, in a flash of inspiration, creates a masterpiece on the first try. My consciously constructed habits and routine are, however, exactly how I steer the flow of creativity into manifestation. The more I've practiced what works for me, the more free I am to then work intuitively. The mechanics of my established and trustworthy process submerge, and my free-wheeling, intuitive self can rise up. I'm free to experiment, change directions, or focus sharply. My process creates a structure where my imagination, creativity, and magic can soar.

Although the process is methodical, I am flexible. I change or abandon it (or parts of it) according to what the project asks of me. When an idea springs from my vision so complete that no tweaking or test runs are necessary, or past experience has taught me exactly what I need to know, I skip the prototypes. My goal is to use the most elegant process I can to get those beads dancing to my music.

Critical to tailoring a reliable, workable process is knowing yourself—your needs and wants, your strengths and weaknesses. What degree of chaos are you comfortable with? Do you like your studio clean? How do you like your materials organized? Do you enjoy the accompaniment of silence, music, or noise? Are you easily distracted? Do like to work under a certain amount of pressure? Do you need to be relaxed? For how long a span of time can you do your best creative thinking? Your best meticulous producing?

Creativity, motivation, productivity, and efficiency are not constants; they ebb and flow. The time of day or night you work is critical. I treat the hours when I'm well rested and focused as the most precious of the day. This is the time for whole-hearted concentration, creative thinking, and working. When I have physical energy but am not at peak mental alertness, it is production time: I handle repetitive or pre-planned tasks that don't require creative decisions.

Pages 138–141 describe the processes other jewelry designers have developed. What of their methods can you incorporate to make your process a more fertile ground for your imagination and creativity to flourish?

THE GAP

Have you ever been frustrated by the fact that the piece you just finished is not as spectacular as the vision of it you held in your mind? Let's talk.

The gap between vision and its manifestation is as old and ever-present as human expression itself. Our plans, dreams, and imaginings never turn out exactly as we envisioned. Sometimes they fall short. Sometimes they turn out better than the vision. This is the way of creativity, the way of life. It took me years to learn to deal with what I call "the gap" in a healthy way and realize it is simply part of the creative process.

Every piece we make is a snapshot in time. Every masterpiece ever created could have been different, possibly better. When I came to peace with this I found an invigorating freedom. I was free from guilt and self-recrimination. I was more compassionate with myself. I still grapple with it. But each time I can lock into this more healthy perspective—I know it's healthy because it energizes me—a peace that's both exhilarating and relaxing settles in me.

Although it's frustrating, a piece that doesn't match your vision does not indicate failure. Depending on the nature and size of the gap, it could

mean you need to improve your skills. Or maybe you need to rethink the vision. Or perhaps you need an entirely new vision; maybe now isn't the time for this one, or maybe it was not quite yours to begin with. Or it could simply indicate that you know more now than you did when you set sail on this particular journey.

Look as objectively as possible at the gap. Decide what contributed to it—lack of knowledge, expertise, or materials? Assess its size and scope and decide what you're going to do about it. Have you learned what you need to from this piece and is it time to move on? Or are there lessons to be

Mary Hicklin
Abalone Leaf Necklace,
2010
Centerpiece: 6 x 5 cm;
Length: 48 – 64 cm
(adjustable)
Depth: 0.6 cm
Abalone, freshwater pearls,
faceted pearls, Chinese
freshwater "keshi" pearls
cable, sterling silver;
stringing
PHOTO BY ARTIST

Candie Cooper
Orient Express, 2007
19 cm
Glass beads, charms, metal chains, silk;
wire wrapping
PHOTO BY STEWART O'SHIELDS

learned in re-creating it? There are many ways to proceed, but judging yourself as non-creative, hopeless, or a failure just because the gap exists isn't one of them. That path drains your creativity.

We're always trying narrow the gap between vision and execution. That is often exactly what we need to do, what we're supposed to do. However, on the creative journey, that is not the ultimate goal. The ultimate goal is to express what you wanted to express with the piece, and learn what you set out to learn. The most important questions to explore are: Did I say what I wanted to say and learn what I set out to learn? How has it changed me? How am I different as a result of this latest creation?

Let yourself be changed by creating. See the process as your teacher.

At its essence, creating art is a path to the sacred. It is about growing and learning. It opens us to ourselves. It spurs us on our spiritual journey. The gap is part of this sacred process. Falling short is part of the growth, as much of a teacher as success.

The purpose of the gap is so we continue reaching. Humans always strive to become more. As we grow, so our imagination and vision for what we want to create grows. We then must develop the skills to keep up with that part of us that is stretching into new territory. Creativity is an upward spiral of growth and realization. I can't imagine anything more fun!

Sarah Shriver
Art Nouveau Bracelet, 2009
Beads 4.4 x 1.2 cm
Polymer clay, elastic
PHOTO BY HAP SAKWA

FEAR, DOUBT & THE CREATIVE PROCESS

Fear and doubt are both part of the creative process. Let's examine each, beginning with fear, for whether we are novice or master, fear will accompany every artistic creation we care about.

Fear

As I sit down to write this chapter, my notes in stacks of colorful index cards, I find myself fidgeting. Getting up for another glass of water. Checking email again. And again.

Ah! I recognize it. Fear, on cue, sat in my chair ready to work before I did. After decades of creating, it can still take me by surprise, for it is far more punctual and diligent than I. It makes its presence known in seemingly insignificant ways: I think my desk needs cleaning again, the chair needs adjusting, and there aren't enough ice cubes in my water glass.

And then I remember to enact my ritual. It's become a ritual because each time I get to the heart of what I'm creating, fear returns. The more passion I feel, the stronger my fear.

I admit it: I'm scared.

So begins the ritual, the dance fear and I share as partners. I extend my hand, invite it out of the shadows into the light where it has less power over me.

We clasp hands and I smile. "OK, let's hear it." I give it a little twirl.

You think you know what you're going to write, it declares, *but you don't. You think it'll make sense, but it won't. Are you sure you want to do this? You're gonna regret it. You'll make a mess,* it shrieks, reminding me of past failures.

I touch my index finger to my lips, shushing it. "You know the rules, we only talk about this moment, this here, this now."

Yeah, well, OK, but… but… It falters, then regains equilibrium. *This will be the time. This time will prove what a failure you are.*

"All lies," I reply. "You're saying nothing new, so you have five more seconds, then you will leave."

(There's nothing to be gained by negotiating with fear.)

It won't give up. Its voice rises in pitch. *You can't do this, this will be a disaster!*

I drop its hand, whirl it around by the shoulders and shove it out of the room. I shut the door and turn the lock.

A pristine, spacious silence opens. It's just what I need to hear my own voice, just what I need to let my passion roam freely, playfully.

I know fear will return, even though I won't consciously unlock that door. When I get excited about the next phase, or the next creative decision that must be made, it'll be there. And we'll dance our little dance. And if it has anything new to say, I'll listen because it could be valuable. It could lead me in a new direction, or remind me of something I've overlooked. But most often the fear that accompanies my creativity repeats the same threats it has since childhood. So I consciously show it the door.

When I deny my fear and forget my ritual, fear begins to influence my creative decisions. I take fewer risks. My fear-based choices are always the weakest ones.

Knowing what fuels your fear of creating art helps tame it. In the heart of our fear lurks some kind of threat. Perhaps threat of loss, exposure of a weakness, humiliation, pain, or judgment. If you can identify it, you can look this threat squarely in the eye and realize it is probably a phantom. If your creation turns into a mess, that doesn't mean you are weak, untalented, or a failure. If others judge you, you can handle that; it isn't **the end.** When you're conscious of what is being threatened, fear has less power.

Also, consciousness invites you to learn from your fear. And as you learn from it you can reduce it. As you reduce it you can move beyond it and rise above. Fear need not control your art.

Kristy Nijenkamp,
Untitled, 2010
56 cm
Dyed agate, sterling
silver; stringing

Doubt

Easier to work with than fear, doubt can become an artistic partner. It's important for me to know whether I'm dealing with fear or doubt so I can handle it properly. The difference is in the intensity of the feeling. Within fear is a threat. Fear can stop me. Doubt, however, holds no threat. It causes me to hesitate.

I like to dialogue with doubt because it has much to offer. When it says *I doubt you can do this,* I say "What if I can?" or "If I can't do it this way, what if I try it a different way?"

Doubt, when faced head-on, is a flexible springboard that allows me to see differently, to approach the challenge from a new angle. It often nudges me to pay more attention and look deeper. Once I realized this, I welcomed doubt with listening ears. But I don't get mired in it.

You can turn *I doubt I'll ever be able to design spectacular pieces* into "What if I learn all I can about design and commit to creating a necklace a week for three months? What will will that teach me about myself?"

If your doubt says *I doubt I can design a necklace that this client will love,* find out exactly what the client loves and specifically why she loves it. This doubt can easily be handled by using the Customer Preference Form on pages 128–129.

If you hear *The colors I choose are boring, I doubt I'll ever be able to make dynamic color harmonies,* transform it by asking "What if I choose one color and work with it for an entire month using paper, pencil, crayons, fabric, and beads and get to know it intimately? I'll pair it with other colors in all kinds of combinations until I find 10 that I love. Then I'll do the same process with a different color next month!"

Rebecca Starry
QWERTY, 2012
30.5 x 12.7 x 1.7 cm
Seed beads, typewriter parts, assorted findings, ribbon; bead embroidery, right angle weave

DO YOUR WORK

Every once in a while, after the ritual dance is over, when I feel that sacred exhilaration that comes from manifesting a piece more beautiful than I had envisioned, I sense the dark, raptor-shaped shadow circling the periphery of my mind—my fear has returned. It's closing in for the kill. When it comes at me like this, I stop and call for help. My superhero is neither bird nor plane. It is my copy of the book *Art & Fear: Observations On the Perils (and Rewards) of Artmaking* by David Bayles and Ted Orland. Within a five-minute reading of the dog-eared pages, I'm grounded back into myself, remembering that my journey is more about art-making than end results. I've shared some of Bayles and Orland's most valuable insights below.

My job is to do my work, make my art. Yours is to make your art. Each failure and each success contributes equally to the evolving artist and human being we are and are becoming.

Uncertainty is the essential, inevitable, and all-pervasive companion to your desire to make art. And tolerance for uncertainty is the prerequisite to succeeding.

...every artist must learn that even the failed pieces are essential.

...art is all about starting again.

Between the initial idea and the finished piece lies a gulf we can see across, but never fully chart. The truly special moments in art-making lie in those moments when concept is converted to reality—those moments when the gulf is being crossed. Precise descriptions fail, but it connects to that wonderful condition in which the work seems to make itself and the artist serves only as guide or mediator, allowing all things to be possible.

Artists' Ways

Sherry Serafini

My process begins with the inspiration of a focal point, which could be a stone or interesting button. The colors flow from these elements and are incorporated into the rest of the chosen piece.

My Fridays and Sundays are devoted to free beading, meaning "Don't call, don't email, and don't talk to me." I dive into my work and don't come out until I can't see the beads anymore. I work best in the morning before the rest of the world has woken up. I love the quiet. Occasionally I'll listen to some music or put a favorite Bette Davis movie on.

The other days are dedicated to putting projects together for classes.

Sherry Serafini
Monster, 2012
20.3 x 35.5 x 2.5 cm
Seed beads, crystals, pearls, wire, suede, beading foundation;
bead embroidery
PHOTO BY ARTIST

Frieda Bates

I'm often inspired by a compelling focal bead or stone—and that becomes the beginning of a set of jewelry. I place it in a dish. When I find something that goes with it, I put it in the same dish. I keeping doing this until I have enough colors and shapes to work with. This can take as long as a year. I then lay them out and start moving the pieces around, like a puzzle, until I find the composition I like.

I bead every day, even when traveling, sometimes all day and night. I especially enjoy designing in the quiet of late night.

After 50 years of beading it is in my blood and I love to pass on what I know. I teach beading at the senior center. It is one of my greatest joys to see the looks on my students' faces when they finish pieces that they didn't think they could. When they wear them, they glow. It's a wonderful feeling to know I helped them.

Frieda Bates
Volcano, 2012
49 x 25.4 x 1.9 cm
Handmade dichroic glass cabochons by artist,
seed beads, freshwater pearls, glass beads;
bead embroidery

Marcia DeCoster

I find my creativity flows most freely when I'm not in my usual surroundings. Although much of my beading is done in my San Diego home studio outside on the veranda, my designs are usually developed while traveling. Once a design is developed, I fine-tune it by creating several versions. This stage is usually done at home and results in spurts of non-stop beading.

Many of my designs are conceived when playing with the beads: A familiar component works itself into a new style when I change up bead sizes, types, and colors. A three sided triangle becomes a four sided square with the addition of one repetition. Since much of my work is component based, play brings about new configurations and connections, leading to new design. I've learned never to design when it feels forced. Those are times I take care of other aspects of the business.

I'm inspired by vintage costume jewelry and the work of jewelry artists in other mediums. Often a shape or a color in a piece of metalwork or lampwork will bring forward a vision I want to create in beads.

Marcia DeCoster
Vienna, 2012
Focal element: 13 x 5 x 0.5 cm
Crystal pearls, crystal bicones and seed beads;
cubic right-angle weave
PHOTO BY ARTIST

Barbara Becker Simon

I'm in my studio seven days a week during most of the daylight hours. My creative energy is not so hot after dinner! I try to get all my "administrative" stuff done first thing in the morning. I really want a clone to do this!

I don't always know what I'm going to do in the studio, but being there, in place, causes action, just like Pavlov's dog. I end up working on *something* because I have many projects going at the same time. Getting sidetracked is a given, and often, it's a good thing that will lead to discovery.

When working in metal clay or at the torch, I love listening to audio books (my brain will not let me do this when I am designing, though.) I listen to classical or jazz while I work. Silence in the studio is OK too.

I absolutely need a clear block of undisturbed time (two to four hours) to work. No popping in and out to get the mail, answering the phone, etc. I need this condition to focus fully, otherwise I make no progress.

Different conditions influence the birth of an idea. And they often occur outside the studio environment in situations when I'm doing something completely unrelated, such as driving, waiting at a stoplight, washing dishes, or exercising. The area of my brain that creates is free to frolic while I'm occupied by a mundane task.

Barbara Becker Simon
Study in Grey and White II, 2004
55.8 cm long
Lampworked glass beads, fine
silver beads
PHOTO BY LARRY SANDERS

Jamie Cloud Eakin

The most important lesson I've learned about my personal creative process is to pay attention to my muse. She is fickle and tends to pop up at any time. In the past, when it wasn't an opportune time, I would lament

"Oh no, not now! I'm too busy … later!" Now I've learned to accept the chaos, and when the muse shows up, I pay attention. To make it easy to capture and remember my ideas, I've placed little notebooks around the house. Later I collect these into my main sketchbook. When inspiration strikes, I do my best to let it flow and honor it. This has helped me nurture and promote a creative mindset.

I keep promises to myself about beading time. I try to do something bead-related each day. It might be assembling beads for a project, reviewing my sketchbook, stroking the beads, or cleaning up the studio. When other things in life take precedence and I don't get into the studio, I promise myself bead time. And I keep my promise! My favorite is an entire day of beading, usually on a Saturday. I alert my hubby that I need a "pizza day." That's a day when the only other person I see is the pizza delivery man. No cooking, phone, computer. Just beading. Since I keep my promises to myself, I can have confidence and relax when my creativity gets delayed. Frustration and pressure are a creativity killer for me, so I do my best to keep them from imposing on studio life.

Jamie Cloud Eakin
Spirit Dance, 2011
39 cm long
Turquoise, chalk turquoise,
mother-of-pearl;
bead embroidery

Heidi Kummli

I find inspiration everywhere...sometimes I have too much. Nature inspires me: A walk in the woods shows me moss colors, a circling hawk, or the beauty of her peace. Causes I am passionate about inspire my jewelry: to protest the killing of whales I made a piece that honors the whale, also known as the Manna or mother.

I lay my cabochons and other components, such as porcelain or bone animals, in an empty tray and start placing different stones and components together like a puzzle, seeing what pieces complement each other. I usually lay out five or six different necklace arrangements. If I have smaller stones that match, I'll lay them out for earrings. I can easily stack and store the trays of works-in-progress.

I bead every day. I'm most productive in the morning after the family has gone to work or school. This is my peace time: my time to myself. If I have a large order I need to focus on, I'll listen to a CD, a book, or spiritual teacher. This keeps me in my seat rather than getting distracted.

I never design if I don't have the time or am not organized. Creativity is not a process to rush, but to cherish and honor, for this is a time when we are at one with the universe, letting our spirit be free to express itself through our hands.

Heidi Kummli
Never Cry Wolf, 2012
7.6 x 16.5 x 1.9 cm
Seed beads, porcelain wolf by Laura Mears, silver spoon handles, cabochons, fur, PMC; bead embroidery
PHOTO BY ARTIST

Diane Fitzgerald

Like radio waves, inspiration is out there, everywhere. All we need to do is adjust our minds to tune in and receive it.

I'm constantly on the lookout for new ideas that can be transformed into beading. Sometimes it might be a color combination, other times an interesting shape or juxtaposition of things that click and start the wheels turning. It could also be new beads with new colors, shapes, or finishes. Often my brain is working while I sleep,

and when I wake up, there is a message waiting for me—how to manage a complicated assembly or some other new idea.

I bead almost every day, usually from when I get up until 10 a.m. and again after dinner until 10 or 11 p.m.

I'm never "not designing." The beading muse is always sitting on my shoulder ready to play and at least a part of my brain is always focused in that direction.

Robin Atkins

My creative process begins with something I find compelling, like a new bead or intriguing color scheme. I rarely plan a whole piece. Starting with the initial urge, I simply do the next thing I know. Even without a visual concept of the eventual piece, there is always one more step I can take in its completion. I trust my intuition, not allowing intellectual judgments to get in its way.

In this "improvisational" approach to design, I follow intuitively from one step to the next. The results are definitely more likely to please me than when I pre-plan the piece in my mind. In addition to enjoying the spontaneity of working without a plan, the jewelry seems more original.

I find there is always an ebb and flow to my creativity. Sometimes no amount of self-discipline gets my mojo going. Other times, I find myself in a multiple-day marathon of beading, stopping only briefly to eat or sleep. I cherish the creative periods, and have learned to relax when the muse ebbs away, giving me time for the mundane tasks of life.

When I have to produce on schedule, like for a show, one thing that helps is to allow myself to work briefly in some other art form. For example, I may write a poem or take some nature pictures. Once there's a little spark, I can flow seamlessly into a beading project.

Diane Fitzgerald
Caribbean Blossom Necklace, 2010
45.7 x 1.9 cm; flower 7.6 x 12.7 cm
Crystals and pearls, cylinder seed beads, clasp; netting, sewing
PHOTO BY ARTIST

Robin Atkins
Heart Jazz Brooch, 2008
7.6 x 4.4 cm
Seed beads, glass accent beads, charms; bead embroidery
PHOTO BY ARTIST

Pause for a moment. Realize this: jewelry has been made and worn as long as humans have walked upright. Jewelry is an important part of our lives. It matters. And as a designer you are contributing to this human connection that spans centuries. What you give of your unique voice matters.

We design jewelry not only with our eyes and hands, but also with our hearts. Aim to design jewelry that speaks of who you are, that speaks of the way you see the world, that expresses what you want to say and give to the world.

What are the recurring themes in your life that influence you, the creative artist? If you're unsure, think of novels and movies that touch you deeply. What are their essential themes? For me, the motif of light emerging from darkness has woven itself through my life. I'm drawn to finding hope where there seems to be none, discovering treasures in myself when I've felt there were none. This shows in my use of strong contrasts: a spark of light set against an expansive dark background, light emerging from dark shapes.

While this may seem unrelated to what kind of beads to choose for your next necklace, knowing what drives you does indeed shape all the decisions you make.

I've devised the following questionnaire to help you articulate aspects of your voice so that your art can be a true expression of your inner self. Be patient. Developing your voice is an unending process of self-discovery. As long as you grow and evolve, so will your voice.

Find Your Voice Questionnaire

Where are your strengths and weaknesses as a designer?
Write an "S" on the list if you're strong in this area, or a "W" if you are weak.

___ knowledge of stitches and techniques

___ knowledge of materials

___ knowledge of design principles

___ color use

___ ability to focus

___ ability to let my imagination run freely

___ healthy relationship with my inner critic

___ ability to move self-judgment aside in order to create

___ sense of wonder and curiosity

___ healthy momentum: ability to try again when I don't like the results

___ flexibility of knowing when I either need to learn more or go deeper with my creativity

___ passion for the process

___ passion for the medium and its materials

___ passion for jewelry

___ other

Own your strengths. They are yours. Feel proud! Take the time to think and write down ways you can make your strengths play prominently in your creative process.

Own your weaknesses. In what areas do you want to become stronger? Strategize and write down ways you would enjoy developing and growing. Commit to this strategy with a time limit.

What fires your passion in the following areas? Be specific:

beauty:

form:

design:

interplay of color:

movement:

pattern/texture:

light:

materials:

techniques:

What are the recurring themes in your life that influence you, the creative artist? (Read the paragraphs at the top of this page.)

What stirs your compassion—human rights, animal rights, the environment? In what ways, subtle or obvious, can the depth of your compassion drive, energize, and inspire your creative expression?

You have my permission to photocopy this questionnaire.

WHAT KIND OF JEWELRY
DO I WANT TO MAKE?

WHAT KIND OF JEWELRY
DO I *NOT* WANT TO MAKE?

Ask yourself: What kind of jewelry do I want to make? What kind of jewelry do I *not* want to make? Sometimes the latter is easier to answer.

Here's a list of possibilities; add your own. Circle what appeals to you, cross out what doesn't.

Watch for the patterns that emerge.

If you are well acquainted with your voice, look for things about yourself that you may not have been fully conscious of.

Focus on these two questions with every piece you make. Our voice echoes our different states of being. Come back to this list every couple of years to see if and how you've changed.

I want to make jewelry that makes the wearer feel:

Alluring	Energetic	Luxurious	Showy
Avant-garde	Evocative	Masculine	Silly
Beautiful	Extravagant	Mellow	Simple
Bewitching	Fascinating	Modern	Sleek
Bohemian	Feminine	Mysterious	Smart
Bold	Fiery	Natural	Soft
Captivating	Flamboyant	Otherworldly	Sophisticated
Casual	Formal	Over-the-Top	Spirited
Cerebral	Free	Passionate	Sporty
Charming	Fresh & young	Polished	Subtle
Chic	Friendly	Powerful	Sweet
Colorful	Full of life	Practical	Tasteful
Confident	Glamorous	Precise	Tender
Cultured	Graceful	Progressive	Tough
Cute	Happy	Provocative	Traditional
Delicate	Humorous	Quiet	Unique
Dignified	Intellectual	Refined	Urbane
Distinguished	Intimate	Revolutionary	Vibrant
Dramatic	Intimidating	Rich	Vintage
Dreamy	Jaunty	Robust	Vivid
Dynamic	Lighthearted	Romantic	Wild
Elegant	Lively	Sexy	Womanly
Enchanting	Lovely	Sharp	Youthful

STYLES

What jewelry styles appeal to you. Why?

What styles don't appeal to you. Why?

Here are some possibilties; add your own:

Antique

Avant garde, unusual

Bohemian

Classical Roman

Crafty, handmade

Earthy, natural

Gothic

Grunge

Hollywood glamour

Playful, wacky

Retro

Sleek, understated

Steampunk

Vintage

Challenge Yourself

Art is a two-part dance: creativity (the dreaming and designing) and productivity (the bringing into being). I've noticed that for most artists one is more challenging than the other. Choose your challenge accordingly.

Unleash Your Creativity Sessions:

This challenge is for those who have trouble developing original designs (and those who tell themselves that they can't generate an original design).

Find a photo of a piece of jewelry that excites you. Sit down with a sketchbook, a pencil, and a timer. Sketch the piece loosely—don't get into drawing perfectionism!

Set the timer for five minutes. Sketch the piece again, changing one aspect of the design.

Make at least 10 sketches, each time changing an aspect of the design. Change either the original version, or one of your versions. Push past your limitations. Draw the simplest changes. Draw the craziest changes. Draw the impossible. When you reach an impasse, look at other jewelry photos for ideas. Note: Don't think "I can't draw that because I don't know how I'd construct it." You're only drawing, not resolving construction issues.

   A few ideas to get you started:

   - make one of the beads (or elements) larger (or smaller)
   - color it differently
   - repeat elements (or beads) that aren't repeated
   - add or subtract elements
   - graduate elements large to small (or small to large)
   - add texture and/or patterns
   - add (or delete) fringe, loops, strands, tassels, focal points, spacers
   - reposition existing elements and the space around them
   - change the shape of the focal point or main elements
   - change the movement or rhythm

Try the exercise with photos of jewelry that you don't like. How would you change the design to your liking? Imagine how you would construct one of the "impossible" drawings.

Do this exercise every day for seven days and you'll see, think, and imagine differently. Do it every day for 21 days and you'll be a different designer.

Strengthen Your Productivity Sessions:

This challenge is for those who have plenty of original designs and difficulty manifesting them. Decide you are going to commit to this exercise. This is the most important step.

Get your calendar. Schedule six 45-minute (or longer) sessions a week with yourself for the next three weeks. Write them in your calendar. Ideally these sessions will be at the same time each day, but that's not always possible. If you can only schedule five a week, then so be it. Five is better than none. Schedule a total of 18 sessions.

Session 1: Choose one design and only one (don't let others tempt or distract you during this process). Honor your design by committing to it. Write out the steps for completing the piece in list form. This is your map for the next three weeks.

Keep the map handy, and follow it daily, adjusting where neccesary.

Sessions 2–18: Show up each day and follow your map. Realize that you are important enough to devote this time and energy to your art. You are honoring your creativity, one of the many beautiful aspects of you. This time is a gift to you and to those around you.

When (not if) you become derailed, get back on track without self-judgment and enjoy yourself.

If you finish the piece before the end of three weeks, don't stop this exercise. Go back to step one, choose another piece, and carry on. You're establishing a routine, a process, and a productive habit, which is *far more important* than the finishing of any one piece. Continue to create with joy and pleasure.

About the Author

Margie Deeb is passionate about creativity and beauty. Her personal mission is to keep opening portals to beauty for others and herself. As a teacher she is dedicated to fostering artistic self-confidence grounded in knowledge and unrestrained permission to play. As an artist and writer, she devotes her creativity to self-discovery, healing, growth, and fun. She loves inspiring and being inspired.

She is the first author to publish books on color specifically addressing the challenges presented by working with beads. Her books include the popular *The Beader's Guide to Color* and *The Beader's Color Palette*, which *Library Journal* voted the Best Craft How-To book of 2009. She has published countless print and digital articles on design and color. Margie discussed her approach to color in jewelry on a 2008 episode of the PBS TV show *Beads, Baubles and Jewels.*

Margie is a professional art director, graphic designer, illustrator, and color expert. In addition to her visual arts in pen and ink, oils, watercolor, and charcoal, she is also a musican. She works with all kinds of beading methods, including on- and off-loom weaving and stringing. She is well known for her fantastically colorful loom-woven pieces.

Margie conducts design, color, and writing workshops for artists in all mediums online and throughout the U.S. and Canada. Her art is featured in galleries across the United States and in many books and publications. She offers readers of her newsletter, website, and blog an abundance of inspiration.

www.MargieDeeb.com

Acknowledgments

Thank you, dear reader, for caring about beauty and creativity enough to focus on what I've presented in these pages. Beauty and creativity can—and will—change our world.

Thank you, Darren, my husband, for your unending love, support, and humor.

Thank you, Nathalie, my editor, for all of your valuable contributions and help.

Credits

Editor
Nathalie Mornu

Art Director
Margie Deeb

Illustrator
Margie Deeb

Photographer
Margie Deeb (unless otherwise noted)

Margie Deeb
Untitled, 2012
22 x 22 x 4 cm
Seed beads, Czech pressed glass;
right angle weave, stringing

Contributing Artists

Margie Deeb
Collar of Glass and Light, 2008
22 x 22 x 4 cm
Seed beads, glass dagger beads, vermeil; ndebele, stringing

Debra Evans-Paige
Stingray, 2007
46.5 x 6.3 x 1.5 cm
Stoneware, porcelain, jade, sterling silver, stainless
steel beading cable; hand formed, textured, oxidation
and reduction fired, hammered, knotted

Index

Sarah Shriver
Frida Flower Bracelet, 2011
Beads, 4.4 x 5.7 cm and 4.4 x 4.4 x 2.5 cm
Polymer clay, rubber cord, brass beads; millefiori
PHOTO BY GEORGE POST

Rebecca Starry
Metamorphosis, 2009
10 x 10 x 1 cm
Seed beads, assorted findings, martial
arts throwing stars, fused glass,
assorted hardware, beading thread;
embellished
PHOTO BY JESSICA STEPHENS

PHOTO CREDITS

COVER, LEFT TO RIGHT
Francine Walker
Glacial Pools, 2010
30 x 20 x 0.8 cm
Sterling silver, aquamarine, amazonite, clear
quartz, white agate, yellow turquoise, lime
jade, freshwater pearl, blue topaz, peridot;
soldered, rivited, hammered, wire wrapped,
bezel setting
PHOTO BY ARTIST

Margie Deeb
Untitled, 2007
9 x 3 x 0.5 cm
Seed beads, shell, brass; bead embroidery,
stringing

Stephanie Sersich
Party Necklace, 2010
19 x 20.5 x 2.5 cm
Handmade glass beads and button,
Lucite, glass and stone beads, floss and
waxed linen; knotted
PHOTO BY TOM EICHLER

BACK COVER
Marcy Lamberson
Wristy Business (four floral versions), 2012
Each, 22.2 x 3 x 2 cm
Lampworked glass beads by artist, crystals,
glass pearls, seed beads, sterling silver,
memory wire

PAGE 2
Marilyn Parker
Pansy Ring, 2010
24 x 24 x 1.2 cm
Cylinder beads, glass crystals, lampworked
beads, mother-of pearl, silver

PAGE 3
Kristy Nijenkamp
Spring Fling, 2011
30.5 x 23 x 5 cm
Freshwater pearls, glass, sterling silver, steel
wire, polymer clay, beading wire

PAGE 5
Barbara Becker Simon
Rainbow Chips Necklace, 2006
Length 8.7 cm, largest bead 0.4 x 0.4 cm
Lampworked glass beads
PHOTO BY LARRY SANDERS

PAGE 6
Beth Blankenship
Tidepool Necklace, 2010
Various dimensions
Seed beads, suede-like fabric; bead
embroidery, picot
PHOTO BY JESSICA STEPHENS

PAGE 7
Sandy Lent
St. Pete Beach, 2010
3.8 x 40 x 2 cm
Lampworked beads, sterling silver
PHOTO BY RYDER GLEDHILL